THE GREAT ENTREPRENEURIAL
DIVIDE

The Winning Tactics of Successful Entrepreneurs and Why Everyone Else Fails!

Charles F. Goetz
Michael E. Axelrod
with Josh Kram

Rathskeller Press

Rathskeller Press LLC
2526 Mt Vernon Road, Suite B-324
Atlanta, GA 30338

ISBN 978-0-9799745-0-2

Printed in the United States of America

Cover and Jacket Design by Minava Design.

We dedicate this book to all the entrepreneurs
who keep the economic engine of the
world running strong.

Acknowledgements

As is typical, we would like to apologize to those we have inadvertently left out of this Acknowledgment and thank the members of the Academy (we're not sure which one) for the opportunity to honor those who made this book possible.

Seriously, this book could not have been written without the assistance of so many.

First, our very special thanks to Josh Kram. Josh is a writer who earned his MBA from the Goizueta Business School at Emory University. Josh was kind to accept and undertake the unenviable challenge of helping the two of us write a better, more understandable book. He helped to merge two disparate writing styles. His dual skills were invaluable and his contribution to this book was enormous. Josh has since moved on to work for the campaign of a candidate for President in the 2008 election. We wish him well and know that he will be, as he was for us, a major contributing factor to the candidate's efforts.

We are forever indebted to the scores of highly successful entrepreneurs and industry experts who have given us their valuable time and input. With their help, we have been able to test our theories and prove our conclusions. Simply stated, they have made this a better book. Thank you to all of the entrepreneurs and others who graciously gave of their time. These include but are not limited to: Mike Parham, Eric Hartz, Chad Navis, Andrea Hershatter, Ed Leonard, David Zalik, Mike Fletcher, Howard Gibbs, Harold Enoch, Bert Jones, Byron Kopman, Randall Bentley, Barry Brouner, Ed Rieker, Gerry Benjamin, Harold Solomon, James Davis, Rich Makadok, Marc Lewyn, Gary Ashley, Myrna Goldberger, Massoud Alibash, Jared Hyman, Adam Leaderman, Bob Wilensky, Steve Gorlin, Garrett Van de Grift, Charles Moster, Stanley Tanger, Rob Perkins, Frank Leonard, Elliott Cohen, Steve Fetter, Jeff Leonard, Alan Grodin, Brad Milner, Dan Kohl,

Herb Schwartz, Mike Shott, Ed Hess, Sid Stark, Dean Benamy, Kathleen Shanahan, Eddie Mendel, Alan Bragman and Jack Karcher.

We would also like to thank the students at the Goizueta School of Business who have taken one or more of Charlie's entrepreneurship classes over the past 7 years. With the help of our BBA, MBA and PhD students' questions and feedback, we have been able to enhance the clarity of our findings, rationales and recommendations.

Thank you to Mitzi Navarra who provided her excellent graphic design skills.

To our families who were supportive of this effort and added value all along the way.

Charlie thanks his wife, Gail, a specialist in learning disabilities, whose expertise in Attention Deficit Disorders was extremely helpful in keeping Charlie well focused and on task, and his son, Jeffrey, a doctoral student, whose proofreading of this manuscript was invaluable as were his many insightful suggestions. Thanks also to Charlie's daughter, Ariel, a budding entrepreneur in her own right, who provided insightful suggestions as she pursues her college classes in business.

Michael thanks his wife Lillie, an executive in the insurance industry who provided a great deal of practical insight, experience and contacts with entrepreneurs, and his son Jason, a future journalist, who also provided proofreading help. Michael's son Andy would have helped but he had better things to do.

Finally, Charlie and Michael want to thank you, the reader. This book was written as a way for both of us to give back for all the fortunes in life we have been blessed with.

Table of Contents

Introduction

There Has To Be A Better Way

More than two million new businesses are started in the United States every year[1] – ranging from mom-and-pop gumball stores to biomedical service firms. Yet in the 1980s, the probability that a new venture would succeed was less than the odds of landing on tails in a coin toss. In fact, on average, a staggering 55% of new ventures failed within their first four years.[2] Since then, thousands of scholarly articles, hundreds of books, and oodles of experts have claimed that they have discovered a better way to achieve entrepreneurial success. There has been an explosive growth in the number of entrepreneurship courses offered in business schools and entrepreneurial experts have taken to the airwaves to peddle their sure-fire approach to becoming a CEO and overnight millionaire. So the entrepreneurial world has made progress over the past 20 years, right? Well, sort of. As it turns out, the failure rate of new ventures today averages somewhere just below 54%. Now that's progress! We know that makes you feel a whole lot better, doesn't it? If you were gambling your life's savings on your business, would you want those odds? Neither would we.

According to most of the books written about starting new businesses, the process is simple. Find a product that people want, sell a lot of it for more than it cost you, and voilà, you'll be able retire to your $10 million home, private jet, and personal chef. If only it were this easy, we'd have much more hair and you would have a lot more free time. But of course, this is not the case, and as a result, we offer you a book about starting a business, not a pamphlet or flyer.

The overwhelming majority of books written about starting new businesses are either too basic that they're not worth your time and

---

[1] Mintel. " Small Business Finance: Startups - US ". May 2005. Mintel Reports. Emory University, Atlanta, GA. 10 Aug. 2007 <http://reports.mintel.com>.

[2] U.S. Bureau of the Census; Administrative Office of the U.S. Courts; U.S. 2 Department of Labor, Employment and Training Administration. www.sba.gov/advo

money, too general that you won't know where to start, or too difficult to use that you'll be left wondering, "So how do I apply this concept to my business?" In teaching MBA students and business executives about entrepreneurship, we were frustrated by the choices of books out there... and so were they. While there are certainly great books that deal with slivers of wisdom on starting new ventures – such as how to develop an innovative idea, how to sell your product, how to attract investors, etc. – there is nothing that fully and comprehensively explains all the moving pieces in new businesses and how those pieces fit together. Sit in a scrap yard with the 2,000 parts to build a car, without seeing the design for how the parts fit together, and you will have an idea of the difficulty inherent in combining piecemeal snippets.

There Is A Better Way
"The Great Entrepreneurial Divide" is different. We dive into not only the nitty-gritty mechanics of starting a business, but also explore the ever-important and almost virtually ignored psychology and philosophy of business and consumers that so many new entrepreneurs dismiss. This book is intended to provide the first-time entrepreneur with tactical and easy to follow steps in combination with the big picture of what ultimately drives success in business.

This book is the product of everything that we have learned from a combined 50 years in the business world – practical tools, best strategies, and tactical lessons – from starting dozens of companies, analyzing highly successful and failed businesses, and gathering the collective wisdom of other serial entrepreneurs. From start to finish, we will show you how to do it right. We'll point out what the major obstacles will likely be, how to get around them, and how to use our successes (and failures) to ensure that your entrepreneurial jump is lighter on the risk, heavier on the reward. Many of the sections in the book can easily be entire books in their own right, but we've honed in and highlighted the insights and lessons learned from successful entrepreneurs.

Like our business ventures, we wanted to get this book right the first time. We spent thousands of hours analyzing the inner workings of successful new ventures, meeting with and interviewing serial entrepreneurs, and conducting primary and secondary research to develop a complete yet accessible approach to building businesses. We threw our findings into the fire by applying these ideas proactively to new business opportunities and presenting to our MBA students and business executives. We discovered not only that these findings stood strong, but that we were able to predict with great accuracy whether or not a new venture would be successful.

As it turns out, there are measurable, demonstrable and drastic differences between successful entrepreneurs and their less successful counterparts. Successful entrepreneurs do things differently – and that makes all the difference.

So, Who Are These Serial Entrepreneurs Anyway?

No doubt that when hearing the phrase "serial entrepreneur," your mind wanders to images of Hannibal Lecter or other serial killers, but as far as we know Sam Walton and the Son of Sam didn't have anything in common. Serial entrepreneurs are those entrepreneurs who start more than one business over their career. Whereas entrepreneurs of past generations (the Rockefellers, Vanderbilts, and Carnegies) and contemporary entrepreneurs (Bill Gates and the Google boys) successfully built single companies, serial entrepreneurs successfully build multiple businesses. This is incredibly rare. Of the minority of entrepreneurs that do succeed, the chances that they will succeed again on their second, third, fourth, or fifth (let alone ninth, tenth…) attempt get smaller and smaller with each business. Call us gluttons for punishment, but serial entrepreneurs keep going back for more. Sometimes we've profited, other times we haven't. But over the past 20 years, having started and invested in dozens of companies, we've learned how to do it right and want to give your new business the serial entrepreneur's advantage.

This Is Hard Work

Here's the thing with starting a company: It is hard work. Just because we're going to lay out a proven process for building a successful company does not mean that anyone and everyone can do it. If our book was a product, it would have a big red sticker on it that said, "Warning: Use with Caution" because this isn't intended to be the Cliffs Notes®, easy answer version of entrepreneurship. This is unabridged. Following this path requires patience, exertion, and discipline. We want to give you stuff that you can really act on (after all, you've paid for it). This includes maps and processes that we've developed that will walk you through the dos and don'ts of building your own successful business.

Here's the most common trap: Often entrepreneurs are so enamored of their idea and in such a hurry to get to market that they aren't interested in following a prescribed and orderly path. If you want a greater shot at success, however, the familiar adage applies: Slow and steady wins the race.

We'll show you the way, but you've got to do the work. That's the quid prod quo, the deal, our little agreement. Many of the steps require some homework on your end – through research, analysis, and thinking about how your product fits in with the concepts we're presenting. We hope you won't read passively but will constantly think about how to relate it back to your product and business.

Here's a little secret: This isn't rocket science. We teach graduate business students, and when they come into our class, mostly they're relieved that they don't have to be econometricians, or calculus mavens, and they don't even have to memorize hardcore finance formulas. The math in this book is never anything above high school algebra. We'll noodle around with some ideas and give numeric examples, but being an entrepreneur isn't about being a mathematician. In fact, psychology is more relevant in new business ventures than statistics, economics, and finance combined. If you're anything like our students, you're probably breathing a sigh of relief right now thinking about all those math classes that you slept through.

We Know You Because We Are Just Like You

We know that you lie awake in bed dreaming about your idea. We know that you're fired-up about the notion of being your own boss and owning your future. We also know that you're scared (and rightly so) of the risks. We know because we're just like you.

The "we" perspective in this book is a little misleading because "we" are very different from each other. We have different experiences, different backgrounds, and approach entrepreneurial ventures each in our own way. We also have very different personalities and voices that will come out throughout the book. One of us has been called a "wacky mad scientist" who constantly pushes the limits in new ventures; and, the other has been labeled "far too serious" and a "by the book stickler for detail."

Let's see if you can figure out who is who.

Charlie

"With the toss of my toupee into my boss's face, I knew that my days as an executive at a large corporation were rapidly coming to an end (not to mention that my secret was now out). The entrepreneurial world was calling, as it had since my first lemonade stand, and I was just waiting for the right opportunity. I left corporate America to start building my own empire. My first stop was Paris Fries, a French fry joint in three mall food court locations. It was everything I wanted: exhilarating, creative, challenging, and best of all, I was now in control of my own destiny... or so I thought... Now twenty years later and after 9 businesses in six different industries, I can now honestly say that I have earned my hairline."

Michael

"I practiced law for 22 years and worked with clients large and small, private and public, in industries ranging from healthcare and manufacturing to service businesses and venture capital. From these clients I met successful entrepreneurs and learned what they believed worked and what didn't. I also served on the board of directors of a public company and led the board of directors of two non-profit organizations. After 22 years it was time to move on and I have gotten involved in an array of businesses, investments and teaching, and more importantly, I haven't looked back. Well, that's not totally true. I now look back and realize just how funny the lawyer jokes were..."

Needless to say, it's not hard to distinguish between us. Yet our differences have truly contributed to our successes. We've been partners for a long time now – starting companies and making investment decisions together. We've challenged each others' assumptions, called out each other's bad ideas, celebrated the good ones, had a lot of laughs, and ultimately developed better products and companies at the end of the day. And we haven't killed each other yet.

Your Virtual Business Partner

This book is designed to be your virtual business partner. It asks the tough questions about your business's strategies and tactics, encourages you to look at an opportunity or challenge through a different lens, and pushes you to apply new methods and frameworks to your business concept. While this business partner might be slightly less talkative than your previous associates, jammed into the pages are the voices of serial entrepreneurs who share lessons learned, insightful narratives, and practical tools to help bring your ideas to fruition. Regardless of whether you're starting a sandwich shop or building a bio-technology company, these concepts and ideas will spark your entrepreneurial spirit and demonstrate a better way to build your business and achieve your goals.

Just Do It

Despite the many challenges that come with being an entrepreneur (and there will be many), the payoff is well worth it. Building your own business is the best way to make positive, enduring change in both your personal and professional life. As an entrepreneur, you control your own destiny in a way that your friends climbing the corporate ladder can only dream of. From the upside of fame and fortune and the freedom from a desk job to the ultimate control that you have in your own life, entrepreneurship offers an exciting journey to the life you've dreamed of.

How This Book is Laid Out

This book walks you through the stages of starting a business – from harvesting that spark of an idea that keeps you awake at night to the realization and launch of your business. It is designed to be a step-by-step guide and provide you with tips and tools at every step along the way. While each section of the book can stand alone, the concepts and tools build upon each other from chapter to chapter and this book is intended to be an all-inclusive handbook from start to finish.

Chapter 1: Beware of the Minefields: The 3 Big Reasons Why New Ventures Fail

Insufficient cash on hand, deficient sales, and bad management are the primary culprits for failing new businesses. What are the signs of these problems and how can you avoid them?

Chapter 2: Are You Crazy? Thinking like a Serial Entrepreneur

Getting up to speed in an entrepreneurial world. The six tools that will help you from start to finish: Ask questions, be nimble, focus only on what's important, keep it simple, understand the psychological-emotional dimensions of business, and mapping out your route.

Chapter 3: The Market Knows the Answers You Seek

Using what the market needs or wants to build your product and company. Is your product a high priority? Are there enough potential buyers?

Chapter 4: Does Your Product Shout Value?

Building products that pack a high value punch for prospective customers. How to measure and create value for customers through your product?

Chapter 5: Strategy, Tactics, and Execution, Oh My

Developing a company architecture that enhances your product's value equation. What's the best business model for your company? How can you leverage marketing, sales, operations, and management to provide prospective customers with the most value?

Chapter 6: One for the Money

Completing the final steps before launching the product. How do you build projections, run the business test model, write a business plan, and find backers to fund your vision?

Chapter 7: GO! Getting Off on the Right Foot

Managing your risk to maximize your reward. How do you form a legal entity, cover your ass, set up the company, and hire employees?

Chapter 8: 23 Tips from Successful Entrepreneurs

Tips, tactics, and wisdom from highly successful entrepreneurs.

We wish you the best of luck and we're here to help.

CHAPTER 1:
Beware of the Minefields:
The 3 Big Reasons Why New Ventures Fail

"When I was seventeen, I walked into the jungle.
And by twenty-one, I walked out. And by God, I was rich!"

- Ben Loman, Death of a Salesman

"If you want to be successful, it's just this simple.
Know what you are doing. Love what you are doing.
And believe in what you are doing."

- Will Rogers, Comedian

Watch Out For That Mine!

Starting a business is like weaving through a minefield. A minefield may look deceptively like a beautiful area in the countryside. In truth, however, dozens or even hundreds of mines that can endanger your mission lurk undetectable just below the surface. As an entrepreneur, while no bodily harm will be inflicted upon you if you stumble into these minefields (unless the Corleone Family is your primary investor), these minefields can certainly destroy your business. Just as soldiers are sometimes given maps that point out where minefields are so they won't accidentally step on a mine, entrepreneurs need to understand the terrain around their new venture too. There will always be elements of surprise, risk, and uncertainty that accompany any new business, but knowing what you're dealing with before you get there will certainly help you get through.

Three Easy Ways to Fail

Of the businesses that fail, virtually all of these failures can be attributed to at least one of three reasons: The Company was unable to sell enough of its product, did not have enough cash to pay its bills, or suffered from ineffective management. Sure enough, there are a variety of causes that lead companies into each of these minefields, but sales-related, cash-related, and management-related issues really explain why most companies fail. While these are huge issues, surprisingly most are often ignored by new entrepreneurs – who typically focus exclusively on cash. We'll show you what these issues look like and how to avoid them.

1. *Sales-related issues.* Sales are a company's ability to exchange its product for money in the marketplace. Contrary to popular belief, cash shortfalls are not the main reason why new ventures fail most frequently. In most cases, cash shortages are the result of insufficient sales and the real reason for failure. We may be stating the obvious, but sales are important because they lead to cash, which leads to profitability, which leads to ownership of that big house in the Hamptons that you've been eyeing. While lack of cash is a symptom of a failing company, most often a problem with sales is at the source. What are some of the root causes of sales-related issues?

This is a Great Product – Who Cares?

The Segway personal scootering, transporting, moving thingamabob was going to change the world. Rarely has a product introduction generated so much fanfare. It was so secretive that it had a codename, "Ginger." The press gushed over claims that the Segway was a life altering and life affirming product. The Segway was a solution looking for a problem. So, if your product is not driven by needs or wants in the marketplace or built to be competitive with others in the market, it probably won't have a good chance of selling.

Never Heard Of It

As we write this book, gasoline costs about $3 per gallon. There is a rapidly growing "green movement" looking for ways to reduce carbon emissions in automobiles. Enter Honda with a Honda Accord Hybrid. Great company, logical product, yet it was a huge failure. While the Toyota sold more than 77,000 of its Prius in the first five months of 2007, Honda has sold just 1,700 of its Hybrid Accords.[3]

Like Honda, if your company is not making the sales you anticipated, the problem may be poor marketing. Remember, marketing is intended to educate and drive awareness of the product in the marketplace and the effort is largely based on your ability to pay attention to demographics, psychographics, and all of the other graphics. A poor marketing effort will result in low awareness of your product which will make the job of your salespeople much more difficult.

You Just Can't Convince the Decision Makers

One of the companies we launched sold a product called MedBuddy™. This was a fully-secure method for physicians and patients to communicate over the Internet. Focus group response was markedly positive. However, sales were well below projections. As selling is the physical act of closing the deal, if the salespeople can't persuade customers to buy, sales will suffer. In our case the buyers, mainly physicians and student health centers, had such long sales cycles that our projections were way off. A long sales cycle can result from a number of factors, but a big one is that you have to be able to persuade your prospects to move quickly; otherwise you end up burning cash while you wait for the decision.

---

[3] Kiley, Daniel. "Failure of Accord Hybrid is a Marketing Fiasco." <u>Business Week</u> 05 Jun 2007

We'll Have a 77% Share of the Market Share by Q1

Unless you are setting up a lemonade stand in a drought stricken area, this is probably an overly optimistic projection of sales. Overly optimistic projections can be a killer and they generally result from the fact that the entrepreneur has fallen in love with his/her product and "can't see the forest for the trees." There are several possible consequences. First, if you are building and financing your own business and you are too optimistic with your projections, you'll probably end up closing down or looking for OPM – other people's money. Second, if you are looking for outside capital from funders who know the market, and they think the projections are overly optimistic, not only will you not get funded, but you may not even get a chance to submit a revised business plan.

If I Build It, They Will Come

Not necessarily. This is not an uncommon mistake. While it is often seen as just a problem for retail businesses, a bad location can kill just about any kind of business. For example:

→ If your business depends on employing low wage workers and you locate in an upscale suburban area with very little public transportation, how will your employees get to work?

→ If your business requires highly skilled engineers, how will you attract employees if you locate your business in a grain elevator in the middle of a corn field just because the rent was cheap?

→ If you are a late-night pizza joint located at the epicenter of retirement communities…you get the picture.

2. *Cash-related issues.* Cash is what enables a company to pay their rent, electric bill, employees – and stay in business. As we already discussed, without cash, the business is effectively choked of oxygen. While sales-related issues are usually at the core of a cash-starved company, there also are others reasons for cash shortages.

The Beggar's Cup

A company that is inadequately capitalized from the get-go has no chance. While entrepreneurs typically overestimate how much product they can sell, they often underestimate how much money they'll need at the outset. Here are two typical scenarios:

→ The founder of the small business ends up tapping out all of his credit cards, getting the maximum second mortgage on his house and alienating all members of his extended family by continually asking for money.

→ The operating business obtains 3rd party financing and fails to get enough capital to provide a cushion.

Our general rule is that when you are estimating the cost of starting up a business, calculate your cash needs as best you can, and then increase it by 30%. We are pretty confident that you will fail to "guestimate" the company's burn rate accurately so you'll need the cushion.

The Check's In the Mail

Sales do not immediately turn into cash unless you have a business that requires payment to be made at the time of service like a restaurant. Many businesses will find that there's a time lag between the sale and the payment. In the meantime, you'll need cash because the power companies we know and the employees we hire won't accept accounts receivable as payment. Today, the average customer pays their bills 60 to 90 days after receiving the invoice. Here is where the difference between sales and cash flow really shows up and if customers pay slowly or fail to pay at all, even though you're booking sales, you may actually have negative cash flows.

We're only $10 Billion over Budget!

Almost all businesses underestimate costs. For example, some weapons systems developed for the military are usually billions of dollars over budget. Okay, an extreme example. For the entrepreneurial upstart company, this problem is often related to changes in expenses that have a direct impact on, for example, pricing your product or service. What if you run a delivery service and fuel costs rise 35% because a hurricane destroyed offshore drilling rigs or a coffee shop when coffee bean prices go up because of drought? Your costs will be over budget and the question will be whether or not you can price your services competitively while remaining profitable. Hint: Remember the cash cushion we talked about earlier.

A Day Late and a Dollar Short

What would the world of personal music players look like if Sony had seen the iPod in its rearview mirror? What would Eastman Kodak look like if it had loved digital media as much as it loved film? Getting to market late, or failure to gain traction, can be a show stopper. No doubt that these companies were forced to overspend just to keep up with their market-leading rivals.

3. *Management-related issues.* Management is the group of people who lead the company and management issues are largely connected to human resources.

You May be Good, But You Ain't Superman

Obviously, your business must have people with the necessary skills to succeed. This is obviously true. But when you get to the point that you need to add employees, you'll find that this is a risky venture because of problems often a founder is unwilling to:

→ Trust others to do their jobs
→ Hire people who can speak truth to power
→ Match market-established wages to attract the best talent

It takes a lot of self-confidence to start a business, but that self-confidence will sometimes have to take a back seat so that you can hire the right people and give up some control.

What do Computers and Soft Drinks Have in Common?

Not much, as it turned out in the case of Apple Computer. Back in 1983, Steve Jobs was replaced as CEO by John Scully, a superstar at Pepsi. The only problem was, even though he was brilliant, he didn't have the knowledge of the computer industry, or a vision for the future of computing, or the marketing genius, like Steve Jobs had. Steve Jobs returned, reignited the company, and now the iPod and iPhone are ubiquitous.

Specialized market knowledge trumps great management and business acumen.

Magic Carpet Ride

Flying by the seat of your pants is a great slogan for a flying carpet merchant in the winding streets of Istanbul. It is a lousy management strategy. The business world can be complicated no matter what business you are in. You'll have direct or indirect competitors who are smart and can and will affect your business. If you don't plan -- through a business plan, projections and the like – there is a 99% probability that your business will fail.

Should You Build a Hotel on Park Place and 3 Houses on Boardwalk At the Same Time?

Monopoly, the biggest selling board game in the world, is a great game because if you over-expand your real estate holdings and go bankrupt there is still beer in the refrigerator. In the real world, over-expanding your business may have more dire consequences. And don't think it is just small businesses that over-expand. Even companies like Wal-Mart, Best Buy and Circuit City either close locations or announce reductions in the number of new stores they are opening on a regular basis.

Over-expansion also relates to management and its ability to control internal growth and growth by acquisition. In the case of buying a business in order to expand, a key question is: Do you have the skills to manage the integration of the two companies, whether integrating computer systems or corporate cultures? Likewise, for a franchisor, a key question is: Do you have the necessary skills to sell new franchises and manage quality control? Do not underestimate the need for proper management skills to handle growth.

We're Not Saying Dennis Kozlowski Stole from Tyco When He Was CEO, We're Just Saying…

Stealing goes on at big companies and at small companies, and it is critical that you take the time to put in the controls to prevent it.

The Sarbanes-Oxley Act of 2002 is a law that was adopted by Congress shortly after the great Enron-Tyco-Qwest epoch. The law requires public companies to put in place internal controls designed to detect/prevent fraud. Congress acted to force public companies to answer the question, "Who's minding the mint?"

Don't think that only large companies should worry about unethical behavior. Failure by a company of any size to put in processes to detect and prevent theft, embezzlement, etc. can be devastating.

They Looked So Good on Paper

Consider the following:

➜ "A" people hire "A" people; "B" people hire "C" people. Hire the "A" people!

➜ Don't assume that your number one salesman can also be a good national sales manager; the two positions require very different skill sets.

➜ Delegate with clear lines of authority.

➜ If there are three equal owners of your business, make sure you know who makes what decisions or how many of the owners must agree on big decisions.

➜ Don't fall for the line: "If you pay me more I'll work harder."

➜ Do you really need to hire your brother-in-law?

The Fallacy of Multiball – Stay Focused

One of the great joys of playing pinball is when you get "multiball." Then all of a sudden, three or more pinballs pop out, lights flash, buzzers and bells go off, and about two seconds later, the balls go into the gutter and you've scored a grand total of 23 points. Ouch. Why did that happen? Because there was so much commotion you couldn't focus.

The same is true for your business. Do you really think you can, at the same time, design the product, arrange for it to be manufactured, develop the marketing strategy, make sales calls, manage the cash, raise venture capital, and so on? Focus is critical.

Ever Heard of Elisha Gray?

While everyone knows that Alexander Graham Bell is the father of the modern telephone, not many people have heard of Elisha Gray, a professor at Oberlin College who developed the same idea as Bell at the very same time. In *Historical First Patents: The First United States Patent for Many Everyday Things*, it was reported that both Bell and Gray went to the US Patent Office on the same day, February 14, 1876, to submit the paperwork to patent their inventions. Bell was submitting a regular patent application, while Gray was submitting what's known as a caveat (an announcement of an invention to be patented). It was later discovered that the device described in Gray's caveat would have worked, while that in Bell's patent would not have. Rumor has it that Gray had completed his paperwork earlier, but simply forgot to submit it. So Graham was the fifth entry of that day at the patent office, while Gray was 39th, and therefore, the U.S. Patent Office awarded Bell with patent #174,465 for the telephone.[4]

---

[4] http://www.oberlin.edu/external/EOG/OYTT-images/ElishaGray.html

CHAPTER 2:
Are You Crazy?
Thinking Like A Serial Entrepreneur

"A pessimist sees the difficulty in every opportunity;
an optimist sees the opportunity in every difficulty."
- Winston Churchill, Prime Minister of the United Kingdom

"Of course I'm crazy, but that doesn't mean I'm wrong."
- Robert Anton Wilson, American writer

Before we get down to explaining the details of how to start a business, there are six important tools that successful entrepreneurs should never leave home without. The need for these tools will arise in almost every phase of business-building and we're going to refer to them time and again throughout the book. Believe it or not, these fundamental ideas are the foundation of what distinguishes the most successful entrepreneurs from the rest of the pack.

1. Ask Questions
2. Be Nimble / Take Action
3. Focus Only on What's Important
4. Keep It Simple
5. Understanding How Emotions Affect Business
6. Map Out Your Route

Ask Questions

Entrepreneurship is nothing like school. In school, it's all about getting the right answers. In entrepreneurship, it's about asking the right questions. All too often entrepreneurs don't take the time before they dive into a new venture to determine what they do and do not know about the business. They tend to overestimate what they do know and ignore what they assume to be insignificant details about the nebulous unknown. Mostly, in their haste to get started, they just skip over this step. Going in without good questions can be dangerous as famed investor Warren Buffet points out:

> "The fellow wanted to get acquainted with folks, so he went over to the village square and saw an old man with a kind of mean looking German shepherd. He looked at the dog a little tentatively and he said, "Does your dog bite?" The old man said, "Nope." So the stranger reached down to pet him, and the dog lunged and nearly took off his arm, and the stranger as he was repairing his shredded coat turned to the old man and said, "I thought you said your dog doesn't bite." The guy says, "Ain't my dog."[5]

Eighteenth century philosopher and thinker Voltaire said, "Judge a man by his questions rather than by his answers." Questions are an important tool to find problems looming around the corner that ought to be avoided as well as opportunities that should be exploited. The existence and scope of problems can come out quickly if you ask the right questions. The goal is to look for trouble by poking holes in your own assumptions and preliminary conclusions. No plan, regardless of how brilliant, is bullet-proof. You'd prefer to know where the "soft spots" are sooner rather than later.

---

[5] Lowenstein, Roger. The Making of an American Capitalist. New York: Doubleday, 1995.

On the flip side, questions lead the way to new opportunities. They enable you to push against your own reality and ask, "Just because it's always been done like this, does it mean that it always will?" Questions can inspire innovation, change, and that spark of genius that makes your product stick out from the rest. If you don't ask, you won't get. Missing out on an opportunity can be a lot more damaging to your company than not seeing a problem.

Don't worry: There's not necessarily an answer to each of the questions that you will ask, nor are you asking them to an all-powerful, all-knowing professor; but, by developing a list of comprehensive and insightful questions, you'll improve your likelihood of future success.

In talking with entrepreneurs, we have found that they tend to ask questions that share these traits:

→ **Comprehensive:** Approach your business with a fresh set of eyes. Challenge what you might assume to be "universal truths" by developing questions that attempt to punch holes in the very fundamentals of your business. By addressing topics such as the market, prospects, competition, finances, operations, product or service, comprehensive questions are designed to ensure that no information which might be vital to the success of the business is left unchallenged. By developing breadth and depth to your questions, you will undoubtedly improve your understanding of the business and better prepare for and prevent surprises. No rock should be left unturned in building a new business.

→ **Creative and Innovative:** Be creative with the questions you ask. Pose the same general questions in different ways in order to identify new perspectives on problems and opportunities. Think about the problem through different lenses – from the perspective of an entrepreneur, a social studies teacher, a 10 year old child. Do not accept the status quo. Challenge conventional wisdom. No matter the issue, a successful entrepreneur does not take anything on faith because there is always a new angle, new perspective, or marginal improvement that can be brought into the equation. We've found that nearly all of the most successful entrepreneurs that we know didn't invent the wheel or the suitcase; they just put the two together. Ask daring questions that challenge "the way it always has been" to find innovation.

→ **Risk-Focused:** Every new venture has risk. The key is trying to be successful with as little risk as possible. Winning entrepreneurs ask questions in order to paint an accurate picture of the risk factors so they understand what they are up against. By identifying the areas of highest risk, you can try to minimize them or factor them in as costs. For example, if you are building a health services company, having considered the risk of reimbursement changes, rising costs of malpractice insurance, and a possible shortage of professionals, you will better be able to build a more fool-proof business plan.

Three more thoughts on questions:

→ While there are no stupid questions, there are bad questions. A bad question is one that misses the "guts" of an issue. For example, you might ask a vendor for the price of a component as you are calculating the cost of building your product (a good question), but because the answer will leave out things such as who pays for shipping, who pays to insure the components in transit, and what warranty the vendor provides, you're getting an incomplete picture.

→ Don't fall into the trap of asking questions to simply validate your idea. If all you're looking for is reassurance that you are wonderful and doing everything perfectly right, go buy Dr. Phil's latest book; instead, use these questions as an opportunity to shoot at your idea and business.

→ Involve others; bring in family, friends, classmates, colleagues to share their own unique perspectives with you. They will naturally come at you with questions that may help you in planning and may come up with new opportunities that you may have never considered.

Charlie

"Don't decide you have the answer and then think of a question to fit it! Carnac the Magnificent, one of the wonderful characters played by Johnny Carson, the famed late night television show host, would hold an envelope up to his forehead and predict the answer to the questions in the envelope. Only then did he open the envelope and read the question. While this backwards approach was good for TV, it's bad for business."

Hopefully this discussion has prompted you to start thinking about questions you need to ask about your venture. Don't worry if you can only think of a few questions right now. Throughout each of the sections of the book, we will offer up general questions that will help orient your thinking and give you examples of the types of questions you might want to ask.

Be Nimble / Take Action

You won't be surprised to hear this – most entrepreneurs are control freaks. Nor will you be surprised to hear this – while you think you're in control, you're really not. In business you can plan all you want (and you should plan), but as is the case in life, reality will undoubtedly force you to deviate from that plan. Your success as an entrepreneur then largely depends on how well you can adapt to the ever-changing nature of business.

Remember:

→ It is easier to change the direction of a jet ski than a battleship
→ You must be able to go from offense to defense and back to offense
→ You have to be able to hit a long drive and a putt

There is certainly no shortage of metaphors, but the point is that you must be nimble in your thinking and your actions. Being able to change directions quickly if you have to, making decisions with minimal information if you have to, and adapting to uncertainty if you have to, is essential to every aspect of your business, whether it is a product change, a new marketing approach, or a change in management.

Coupled with being nimble is the importance for entrepreneurs to take action. We've seen plenty of entrepreneurs who drag their feet, overanalyze a problem, and noodle around with trivial details at the eleventh hour only to get beaten to market (and ultimately beat out) by a competitor. Speed and dexterity go hand-in-hand.

Focus Only on What's Important

Most serial entrepreneurs probably have some form of Attention Deficit Disorder (we are not making a diagnosis but an educated guess based on experience with entrepreneurs). After all, these are people who can't seem to sit still. This ADD is partly what makes them so unique. Their brains are constantly spitting out ideas and coming up with new solutions to old problems. Yet, even these attention-challenged individuals stress the importance of focus, which separates less successful entrepreneurs from their more successful peers.

There are three primary areas where a lack of focus can hurt a new venture:

→ Focusing on too many projects at once
→ Not focusing sufficiently on cash
→ Lack of focus on time management

Focusing On Too Many Projects At Once

Entrepreneurs share an uncanny and natural ability to identify market needs and wants before others and come up with potential solutions. After these flashes of light, entrepreneurs, who are hardwired doers, want to spring into action and implement the solutions immediately. They justify this by saying it helps them to diversify their risk: the more things they have happening, the better their chance that one will prove successful. Yet entrepreneurs so enjoy finding market needs and developing solutions that they tend to end up working on many non-related concepts at the same time. Diversity is helpful, but the entrepreneur should not have more baskets than eggs, either.

Not only did we visit with entrepreneurs who were running several businesses simultaneously, but we did the same thing when we were first starting out. While this may sound like a harmless indulgence, it's anything but. The truth is that it's hard enough to be successful when you have only one thing to focus on at a time, but the more balls you are juggling at any given time, the less likely that all of them will stay in the air. Instead what usually happens is that most of these businesses barely get off the ground and even if one does, the entrepreneur is reluctant to kill the other projects. The result is that businesses with the most potential never receive the attention and resources they deserved.

Not Focusing Sufficiently on Cash

Cash is the most important factor that determines whether a company sinks or swims. Recall that one of the three minefields mentioned at the outset that can crash a business mentioned at the outset was related to insufficient cash on hand. When a company runs outs of cash, you might as well shut the door and turn off the lights because you're done. It doesn't matter that sales are rolling and in just a few more months, the business would have, could have, or should have been successful.

Many entrepreneurs mistake profitability for cash when these are very different things. Being profitable only means that the amount of new sales generated is greater than the amount of expenses the business incurs in the same time period. Looking at sales figures alone, however, can mislead you as to how successful you really are. Most buyers usually defer payment or buy on credit. As a result, the average length of time until the cash owed to you is in your bank account can be between 45 and 60 days or more. Consequently, many companies that reach a break-even point (revenues = costs) find that they often need an additional two to three months of cash just to stay afloat. In the end, a check coming your way two weeks from now isn't as helpful as you might think in keeping your lights on and business running today.

The wisdom, "cash is king," never rings more true than in new ventures. As such, it's imperative that entrepreneurs know exactly what their company's cash position is at every moment. When cash gets tight, entrepreneurs no longer focus on building the business, but on paying their bills.

Lack of Focus on Time Management

Time is your most precious resource. While it is always (theoretically) possible to raise additional money, time – once gone – is never coming back. Entrepreneurs typically struggle to manage their time. They tend to dedicate their time to whatever the most pressing need is at that moment. This reactive approach to management means that entrepreneurs spend 90% of their time putting out fires, filling out forms, going to meetings, and essentially focusing on the most immediate tasks while longer-term business priorities and strategic planning are relegated to "when I have time…"

The more successful entrepreneurs religiously allocate specific time within the schedule to devise new strategies and tactics for growing the business. While they still have the same burning day-to-day issues to deal with, they put a higher premium on their creative time.

There are many excellent books available to help entrepreneurs better manage their time, such as The One Minute Manager by Kenneth Blanchard, PhD, and Spencer Johnson, M.D. and The Time Trap by R. Alec MacKenzie. Here are just a few examples of time management tactics:

→ Develop, prioritize, and implement personal daily to do lists
→ Delegate lower value tasks
→ Minimize distractions where possible (i.e., don't take calls or setup appointments for the same 2 hour period each day)

Keep It Simple

Steve Jobs, the CEO of Apple, attributes part of the iPod's success to its simplicity: "Look at the design of a lot of consumer products – they're really complicated surfaces. We tried to make something much more holistic and simple. When you first start off trying to solve a problem, the first solutions you come up with are very complex, and most people stop there. But if you keep going, and live with the problem and peel more layers of the onion off, you can often times arrive at some very elegant and simple solutions. Most people just don't put in the time or energy to get there."[6] Albert Einstein said, "Everything should be made as simple as possible, but no simpler."

From the technology frontier to the design world, products and companies have lived and died by their ability to keep it simple. The idea that simplicity reigns had its origins in 14th century English thinker and Franciscan friar William of Occam, who believed in the "law of succinctness," and is what we know today as Occam's Razor. The modern day and perhaps less ornate equivalent, "keep it simple, stupid," can be linked to the development of the Apollo program in the 1960s.

This concept is a great rule of thumb in literally every aspect of a new venture – from developing products to communicating with customers, employees, and investors. Too often we've seen entrepreneurs over-complicate products and ideas and have suffered the consequences. Remember that people want simplicity whether it's easily accessible information or effortless tools to improve their lives. This idea will come up time and again throughout this book.

---

[6] Levy, Steven (2006, October 15). Good for the Soul. *Newsweek*, from http://www.msnbc.msn.com/id/15262121/site/newsweek/page/0/

Understanding How Emotions Affect Business

We don't want to get all "touchy-feely" here, but we've found that there is a huge emotional component that blankets almost every aspect of starting a new business. Risk, fear, opportunity, and reward all play a huge role in explaining the behavior of everyone with whom your business will interact with – customers, employees, investors, and even yourself. As such, it's not just enough to be a math maven and number cruncher extraordinaire to be a successful entrepreneur; it's just as equally necessary to be an amateur psychologist.

Daniel Kahneman, a Princeton psychology professor and Amos Tversky, a Stanford psychology professor, won the 2002 Nobel Prize in Economics for their work bringing psychological insights into economic theory to explain idiosyncrasies in decision-making. While economics suggests that people act as rational agents and make decisions solely on the basis of maximizing benefit or pleasure, the duo found that in many cases, people seem to behave "illogically" – yet there was logic to their irrationality.

They found that that people will make different decisions whether they're trying to minimize losses versus maximize gains – even if the total value of the losses and gains are equal. If people perceive more risk, they will naturally choose to avoid or minimize negative consequences.

For example, in an experiment conducted in the 1980s, the psychologists told subjects to imagine the outbreak of a disease that was expected to kill 600 people. They were told to choose between two different public health solutions to fight it. The first option had a 100% chance of saving 200 lives while the second had a 33% chance of saving 600 lives and 66% chance of saving no lives. Most respondents selected the first option – preferring the certainty of saving 200 lives.

Experiment 1:
- → Option 1 has 100% chance of saving 200 lives
- → Option 2 has a 33% chance of saving 600 lives OR 66% of saving no one

Experiment 2:
- → Option 1 has a 100% that 400 people will die (or save 200)
- → Option 2 has a 33% chance that no one will die (save 600) OR a 66% chance that 600 will die (save 0)

When the identical outcomes were framed in terms of lives lost, the subjects' respondents changed dramatically. When told to choose between a solution where 400 people would die and one in which there was a 33% chance that no one would die and a 66% chance that 600 people would die, most subjects chose the second solution, a less certain (and more risky) alternative.

Professor Kahneman explained the results by saying, "The function for gains and losses is sort of kinked. People really discriminate sharply between gaining and losing and they don't like losing."[7]

Much of your job as an entrepreneur will require you to manage emotions. Economists and less successful entrepreneurs argue that if you create the product with the greatest benefits and value, you'll be the winner. But as this example has shown, there are many deeper and more complicated issues that affect human behavior. These non-quantifiable feelings and emotions will continue to come into play throughout your business and will affect almost every single decision that you'll make.

---

[7] Goode, Erica. A Conversation with Daniel Kahneman; On Profit, Loss and the Mysteries of the Mind." New York Times 05 Nov 2002/

Map Out Your Route

We estimate that the average entrepreneur who starts a business and fails within three years spends more than 5,000 hours and $50,000. *We believe that more than 75% of them could have succeeded if only they had a map.* Like any journey, it helps if you know where you're starting out, where you're going, and what you need to accomplish along the way. A map in business is no different from one leading Indiana Jones to the Holy Grail. There are markers along the path to let you know that you're going the right way and forewarnings of the challenges you may encounter. It's critical to plot out a course and develop a plan to get you from your raw idea to the creation of your business. Success doesn't happen by accident.

This example map shows you where this book is going – from understanding the market, constructing a product, building a business, to getting ready for launching your product, and, finally, pulling the trigger. What's more, within each section there are more sub-maps that take you through the processes step-by-step. These maps are intended to be very practical and usable in order to walk you through the various stages of an entrepreneurial venture. Along the way, we'll show you where most entrepreneurs go awry and how to avoid their mistakes. Some of the stops along the way may challenge your ideas and help you build a more effective strategy, while others will point out potential traps that could stall your business. We suggest that you follow the map and go through the recommended steps in order to launch the most successful business possible.

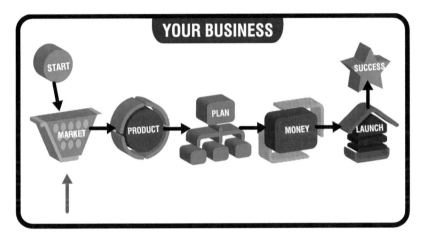

"I never perfected an invention that I did not think about in terms of the service it might give others... I find out what the world needs, then I proceed to invent."

- Thomas Edison, Scientist and Inventor

"I find out exactly what my customers want and then I insist upon it."

- Dennis Crumpler, Successful Serial Entrepreneur

Objective

To determine if there is a sufficiently large market of potential customers who would find your concept attractive enough to justify building your business.

What You Need To Know About the Market

In *Being John Malkovich*, the wacky 1999 hit movie, a puppeteer discovers a secret door that literally leads into the head of movie star John Malkovich. For fifteen minutes, those who pass through the door can see, hear, and feel whatever Malkovich sees, hears, and feels before they shoot out onto the New Jersey Turnpike. In any new business, you must do the same with your market. Find doors that lead into the heads of your future potential customers, your prospects. The most successful entrepreneurs have found these doors and have discovered what it is that their prospects are clamoring for. If you can do this well, your customers will travel to the ends of the earth to buy whatever it is you are selling. Alternatively, many less successful entrepreneurs are so over-confident in their concept that they do not see a need to spend time or money to confirm what they are sure they already know. Many won't realize that they've made a huge mistake until it's too late.

Entrepreneurial success is based on a very simple concept: Give customers what they want and they will knock down your door to get it. The less your product meets their exact requirements, the more you will have to spend trying to convince them that your product is worth buying. The fact is that you will be more successful if you spend the money upfront to discover exactly what it is your prospects want, than you will be spending money trying to convince them that what you have is really what they should want.

With that said we are now going to guide you through the market process, starting from the initial spark of inspiration, through research and market analysis, so that you will be able to determine if your concept has wings.

Where Do Ideas Come From?

Business ideas grow on trees. Well, not really, but they do come from anywhere and everywhere – and often from the most unexpected places. A conversation with a stranger on a plane. Picking apples. Watching bad daytime television. Some entrepreneurs will tell you that they woke up in the middle of the night with a great idea for a new product; others say that it started with a gut feeling about a need that was not being satisfied in the market.

For George de Mestral, a Swiss engineer, it was a walk through a field of weeds. When de Mestral arrived home from a stroll in 1948, he found cocklebur seeds on his jacket. The seeds, barely larger than a fingernail, had hooked spines that stuck to his jacket and were surprisingly difficult to remove. This momentary annoyance gave way to one of the great inventions of the century when de Mestral used the lessons of the burr to create a practical new fastener, Velcro.

So maybe ideas do grow on trees – or at least cocklebur plants.

Don't Be Afraid… Ask the Market

Regardless of where your idea came from, before you even begin building the product[8], you have to go to the market and answer the following two questions:

First, does your product satisfy potential customers' needs or wants?

Second, are there enough people out there who will want to buy your product so that you can turn a profit?

These are absolutely critical questions to answer. Surprisingly, we often see entrepreneurs skip over this step entirely or only barely scratch the surface of the market before they begin product

---

[8] For the sake of simplicity, when we refer to "product" in the text, we really mean products or services.

development. They often miss something important. Maybe your product idea doesn't really satisfy the market or perhaps the concept is a good one, but the market's not big enough. Sure your mother, uncle, and sister will buy it because they don't have a choice, but is that really enough? Velcro might have been a nice novelty, but did it satisfy a need? Was there a market? Perhaps just as wise as de Mestral's invention was his realization that it could be used in lieu of buttons, zippers, and shoelaces. He created a new need, and thus a new market.

What's the Difference between Needs and Wants?

Approximately half the books on entrepreneurship say needs are more important than wants, while the other half say wants are more important than needs. So who's right? In our opinion they're both wrong.[9] We found that needs and wants are equally important. But we're ahead of ourselves.

Entrepreneurial success starts by understanding the needs and wants of the market. So what exactly are needs and wants?

> *Needs* are born from problems. Problems cause pain. The greater the level of pain, the more important is finding a solution for that need. Pain can be something that you're experiencing at the moment, or it can be something you're concerned will happen to you in the future. For example, someone who is bleeding has an extremely high need for medical attention now. Waiting is not an option. Their need to stop bleeding is excruciatingly high. However, a need can also arise from a problem that may occur in the future. For example, safety airbags in cars are sold not because the driver is having a car accident at that moment; they're sold because drivers are concerned about the possibility of an

---

[9] Uh oh: There goes any hope of selling our book to them.

accident in the future. Obviously airbags are not as high a need as bleeding to death, but they're still significant enough that all cars must now be sold with them. Needs are generally quantifiable and the effects of not satisfying them can be measured in terms of time, money, or life/death.

Maslow Knows a Thing or Two About Needs

Abraham Maslow knew what got you going. The first born of 17 children to Russian immigrants in the early 1900's, Maslow became a renowned psychologist and developed a framework for understanding human's hierarchy of needs. He postulated that people have different kinds of needs – ranging from innate needs like food and air at the bottom of the pyramid to creative outlets like painting and playing music at the top. As you might have guessed, breathing air is a higher priority need than painting a picture. And as an entrepreneur, you can stack your concept against Maslow's hierarchy to determine its importance. Products that address personal safety issues will generally have more traction than those satisfying self-actualization.

Wants are interest driven. The more elevated the level of interest, the greater the prospect's desire. Wants tend to be emotion-based and, as such, are not easily quantified, but can range from fear, risk, and a sense of belonging, to personal self worth, happiness, and concern. That doesn't mean, however, that they are any less important than needs. Actually, emotions play a huge role in customers' buying decisions. Just look at the role that wants play in explaining the prices of products. If the product satisfies higher level wants, it's naturally going to command a higher price. For example, if you are looking for a pair of jeans to cover your legs and keep them warm, you could buy a pair that fits well enough from Wal-Mart for as little as $15.00. Why then do people pay well over $150.00 for brands like "7", MAVI or Diesel? While there might be differences in quality between "7" and Wal-Mart Jeans, it's certainly not $135.00 worth of quality. The vast majority of the variance in price can be attributed to these emotional "want" factors. Some buyers suggest that designer jeans make them "look better," feel better about themselves, give them a boost of confidence, or even gain access to what they consider a better social group. Not bad for an extra $135.00, now is it? The more significant the emotional discomfort of not getting or doing something, the greater the desire and more significant the want.

While this may seem like a simple concept, parsing the difference between needs and wants is critical to understanding why people buy and how to sell to them. Most of the time, people have a combination of wants and needs that motivate their choices. Sometimes wants drive the decision; Sometimes needs drive the decision.

Do You Really Need It?
Let's say your reading light just burned out. You have no place else to go inside and it's freezing outside and you have important work to complete.

Clearly, you have a serious need for a new light. What wants drive your decision? You can easily go to a local hardware store and pick up a new light that gets the job done for as little as $5.00 or you can go to a specialty lighting store and pick-up a designer light for $150.00. The two products have the same wattage and both provide light, but one is obviously fancier than the other. If all you really needed was lighting in the room, you wouldn't dream of paying the $150.00. Therefore, your decision to buy in this case is mostly driven by need.

But I Really Want It

Your car breaks down and is deemed unsalvageable. Since this is your only mode of transportation to and from work everyday, you have a high need for a solution to your problem. You have had your eye on a certain red Lamborghini for a long time and while you can't justify its purchase by good gas mileage, lower insurance rates or any other quantifiable reason, you simply want the car because it would make you feel really good. You dream of the way people will look at you in it. You fantasize about who's going to want a ride in it. However, Lamborghini isn't selling because you need a car; it's selling because you want a Lamborghini and the dream that comes with it. Consequently, your decision to buy is purely want driven.

So which is more important needs, or wants?

The Real Reason Why People Buy or Don't Buy: Priority

This may shock you, but competitors aren't your biggest threat in a new business. The biggest threat by far is prospects' indifference. Prospects will have little or no interest in a product if it only addresses a low priority need or want with the related minimal pain or desire. The company can advertise and market all it wants, but these prospects will be focused elsewhere – on problems and desires that have higher priorities in their lives.

The reality is that sometimes needs are more important than wants, but wants can also trump needs. Whether prospects have "needs" or "wants" is not what's really important in building a successful company. What is important is the priority of the need or want. The greater the pain or the more significant the desire, the higher the priority will be. High priority needs and wants are what you're looking for and will be the difference between being extremely profitable or barely limping along.

Here's an example: You could be selling the best carpet cleaning machine in the world at a truly great price, but if prospects have to get their refrigerator fixed, paint their house, get a new air conditioner, go food shopping and save for college, they're not likely to buy your product. Why? Because your product is a low priority for them, relative to the other things that they have to dedicate their resources to first. Even if they didn't have all these other priorities but already had a basic carpet cleaner, their priority would still be low. (This is why it's usually harder to sell a replacement product than a totally new product).

The key to overcoming indifference is to offer solutions for higher priority needs and wants. But how high is high enough? With high priority needs or wants, there is usually a timing element involved. Solutions you need now are naturally going to have a higher priority than solutions that can be put off without significant consequences. If you're bleeding, you need medical attention immediately. If the light in your room burned out, your eyes might hurt and you might get headaches when you read, but you might go a month until you make your way over to the store as other priorities take precedence.

First time entrepreneurs often make the mistake of assuming that all they need for success is a great product aggressively pushed into the marketplace. A great product sells itself, they tell themselves. What they don't realize, however, is that they would have a much better chance of success selling just a mediocre product that satisfies a high priority need or want. These products which customers will pull through the market are much easier to sell than great products that satisfy a mediocre priority.

Measuring Priority

How do you measure priority? This can be a tricky business because you have to get into the heads of the prospects and as you know, human pain and desire are very subjective. Measuring priorities can be part of the primary research you do, particularly through a survey. You will probably have a sense of priority from your business concept and initial research of who your prospects might be. Then you will want to adjust that assumption by considering the widest range of target prospects. That way, you'll be able to compare target prospects with different needs and wants and measure priority relative to one another. This, in turn, will help you select the best market in which to begin selling your product. But be reasonable. If you are building a car, you certainly should not be considering 13 year olds as prospects, but we encourage you to think – within reason – as expansively as you can about who your customers might be.

To help you with this process, we've developed the Priority Identification Chart (Fig. 3-1 on the next page). This simple yet effective tool quickly determines whether a prospect's priority for the specific need or want is worth pursuing. Its purpose is to help you make your first "go / no go" decision on moving forward. Because this isn't particularly rigorous or scientific, a "go" decision only means that your concept warrants investing in market research. A "no-go" decision, however, means that you should go back to the drawing board and reconsider the needs or wants that your product satisfies.

As you use the following chart, here are some tips about each question:
1. **Level.** The higher the pain or interest in satisfying a problem, the higher the priority.
2. **Timing.** The greater the urgency prospects have for a solution, the higher the priority.
3. **Cost.** The less price sensitive prospects are, the higher the priority.
4. **Provider.** The less prospects care about from whom they buy the solution, the higher their priority.

5. **Replacement.** If no solution currently exists, prospects will have higher priority for a solution.

6. Be honest about the answers!

Fig. 3-1

Priority Identification Chart

	Column A	Column B	Column C
1. On a relative basis, how significant is the problem or interest you have identified?	Very Significant	Somewhat Significant	Minimally Significant
2. How important to your prospects is finding a solution to this need or want very quickly?	Very Important	Somewhat Important	Minimally Important
3. How much does the pricing of your product impact whether prospects buy or not?	Not At All	Somewhat	Significantly
4. How important is the company that's selling the product to whether your prospects purchase or not?	Not At All	Somewhat	Very Important
5. Will your prospects have to change from a product they're presently using and previously purchased to use your product?	No	Only Some Will Have To	Most Will Have To

Given the information you already know, for each of the five questions, circle one answer that you believe best describes your market. We understand that you might not know in some cases, but for those just take your best guess. Then score your answers:

- For each answer circled in column A, add 1 point
- For each answer circled in column B, add 3 points
- For each answer circled in column C, add 5 points
- Sum all of the numbers

If the sum is equal to or less than seven, the market you are serving clearly has a high priority; if the sum of your numbers is eight or more, you have to determine how much risk you're willing to accept.

As the sum of your numbers gets closer to 25 your risk increases significantly as your priority decreases.

Do You Have a High Priority for Risk?

Not surprisingly, people adopt products at different times given the level of risk that they are comfortable with. Prospects with a higher priority have more tolerance for risk and are willing to buy earlier to satisfy that priority.

Geoffrey Moore's 2002 book <u>Crossing the Chasm</u> explores how consumers adopt new high tech products and found that there is a "chasm" between the early adopters of a product and the early majority.[10] These two groups, he argues, have different expectations of the product itself and the benefits it will offer them. We want to add to this conclusion and suggest that this pattern is related to priority. The higher the priority, the more willing prospects will be to take risks and adopt quicker. For example, a patient with a rare fatal disease has a very high priority for a cure and as a result will likely try new and experimental options. Innovators don't necessarily need to know that the product will definitely work – they just want to have a shot that it might. Thus, measuring who adopts a product and when is related to the level of a prospect's priority and the risk that they are willing to accept.

Priority Does Not Come Cheap

While it may be possible to increase potential customers' priorities, it will cost more to do so when dealing with lower priorities. On the other hand, higher priorities are better to target from a new product's point of view because the market already understands the need. You'll be able to focus your money on convincing potential customers why your product is better than someone else's; you don't have to spend money to educate potential customers that this is a priority. Whereas a company trying to sell a product in a high priority market

---

[10] Moore, Geoffrey. Crossing the Chasm. 3. New York: Harper Collins, 2002.

need only spend money for sales and marketing related to competition, a company competing in a low priority market first has to spend money to boost the level of priority. The lower the priority, the more money you will need to spend on education and awareness marketing efforts (Fig. 3-2). For small businesses, this is a real danger, because they often don't have the resources to do both and this leads to cash flow issues. As a new business, you'll never have enough money to turn a low priority into a high priority. It's nearly impossible and not worth your time and money. While it is possible to move a medium priority to a high priority, again, this will be extremely expensive. But remember, most of the time, new businesses fail because their products simply don't answer a priority important enough to potential customers. Here's a good example:

Webvan was an online grocery retailer created in the heyday of the internet boom in the late '90s. With $122 million in initial funding and an incredibly ambitious plan to revolutionize grocery shopping, Webvan built mammoth state of the art facilities and distribution systems. Yet this promising idea burned through more than $1.2 billion in two years and declared bankruptcy in 2001.

"In the final analysis, Webvan's demise seems to have had little to do with the quality of the delivery service. While there were, of course, customers who complained of late deliveries and squashed produce, the grocery service generally received favorable reviews from customers," wrote Jonanna Glaser of Wired magazine, continuing, "Webvan's problems never really had much to do with its customers. It was the lack of customers that was the trouble."[11]

"One of the fundamental mistakes that everybody made is the assumption that because there are some problems with the offline experience that everyone would flock online," said Phil Terry, CEO of Creative Good, a consulting firm. Webvan was not able to convince

---

[11] Glasner, Joanna. "Why Webvan Drove Off a Cliff." Wired 10 Jul 2001

people that there was enough discomfort in their current grocery shopping routine and therefore not a high priority.[12]

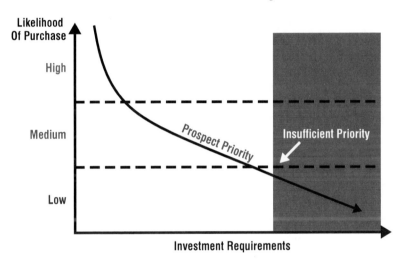

Prospect Priority and Its Impact On Business Investment Requirements

Priority Breeds Attractiveness

As you may recall, the number one reason why new businesses fail relates to insufficient sales. This, in turn, has to do with a product's "sellability."[13] When we talk about sales of a product or service in this chapter, we're not talking about the process of selling, e.g. the sales force, sales people or even sales management. Instead, we are talking about what makes a product or service more "sellable" than others. Sellability measures how many products you are likely to sell based on how attractive your product is and how many people will buy. Sellability is expressed by this formula we developed:

---

[12] Ibid.
[13] Since this is our book, we can make up our own words!

Sellability = Product Attractiveness x Total Qualified Prospects

Let's look at each of these components now.

Product Attractiveness

The more attractive a product, the easier it is to sell. This just makes sense. But what makes a product attractive? From our own experience, product attractiveness is tied to three factors.

Product Attractiveness = Priority x Value x Communication

Since we have already have discussed priority in depth, let's look at value and communication.

Value

Once you determine that your concept satisfies a high enough priority, value then becomes a factor in determining how sellable it will be. When prospects sense that they have a priority, they will search the market for solutions, and to find out what options are available. Value is one of the ways that helps distinguish one product from another. Value is the relationship between a product's benefits and its costs. If benefits outweigh costs, the product has a positive value. While potential customers might not sit down and rationally think about all the components of value every time they make a decision, they do instinctively perform some level of mental accounting to decide whether: to buy or not to buy. We will explain value in much greater detail in Chapter 5 when we show you how to build products that shout value.

Communication

The third component that explains why certain products are more sellable than others is directly correlated to both the quantity and quality of the information a company provides to its prospects. Obviously, a prospect cannot purchase a concept that they don't know anything about. As a result, even a high value product that addresses a high priority need or want will fail to sell if prospects do not know it exists.

We will revisit communication in Chapter 6 when we discuss building your company and effective tactics for "spreading the gospel" about your company and product.

Total Qualified Prospects

While a product's attractiveness is an excellent tool for measuring the likelihood of prospects purchasing your solution, it only tells half the story of sellability. The second half is determining if there are a sufficient number of total qualified prospects to justify building your business. This may sound overly complicated, but "total qualified prospects" is just a fancy way of describing those people or companies who are likely to buy your product. It's a way of estimating the realistic demand for your product. Many entrepreneurs over-estimate how many buyers they'll have which results in disappointing sales and company-wide problems. Knowing what kind of demand you can actually expect will help you project sales and manage the business better.

Here's how you narrow down from all the possible prospects in the world who *could* buy your product, to those who are *actually likely* to buy.

**Total Qualified Prospects =
Total Market Opportunity x Qualification Factor**

Total Market Opportunity

Total Market Opportunity is a measurement of all the potential prospects in your market. Who are your customers? For some businesses, this is obvious. If you are selling a dental product, your customers are probably going to be dentists. With a little research, you'd discover that the total number of dentists in the U.S. as of 2007 (and thus Total Market Opportunity) is approximately 150,000.[14] This represents anyone and everyone who has at least some likelihood of buying a dental product and gives you a sense of the ceiling on the maximum number of potential customers for your business. Needless to say, this is not by any means a realistic indication of the number of customers that you will have. Not all dentists are likely to buy your solution.

For other businesses, the target market (and the resulting Total Market Opportunity) might not be as obvious. We now go from dentistry to orthodontics. One of our companies built a toolkit that helped people with braces fix a lot of common problems with their braces without having to see an orthodontist. While there is only one market for this product – people with braces – we had to choose who our potential customers were. Should we go straight to the end user of the product via the internet? Should we sell it through retail channels in the oral hygiene section? In the end, our research indicated that orthodontists had a high priority for a solution that would free up more of their time and prevent emergency calls requiring them to open their offices on the weekend to fix an errant wire. So we sold the product to the orthodontists around the country – and this insight helped to determine our total market and realistic market.

Qualification Factor

After determining how big the market is, let's now adjust that number based on a qualification factor in order to see a much more accurate picture of how many buyers you can reasonably expect. Most companies use market research to determine what percentage of

---

[14] Bureau of Labor Statistics, U.S. Department of Labor, Occupational Outlook Handbook, 2006-07 Edition

total prospects fit into this category. In the next section of this chapter we will show you how to do your own market research, but broadly speaking, you'll discount the total market opportunity based on qualifications, such as prospects' level of pain, urgency for an answer, price sensitivity, etc. These qualifications relate to both the level of priority as well as applicable demographic factors, such as income, geographic location, etc.

While the number of qualified prospects will give you a much more accurate picture of future sales, how do you know how many qualified prospects you need in order to be successful? It all depends on priority.

The higher the priority that your product satisfies, the fewer qualified prospects you will need. If your customer has a high priority for a solution, this person is much easier to sell to. To sell a product that addresses a lower priority, on the other hand, you may have to make 5-20 times the number of sales calls to achieve the same volume of sales as a high priority product. Let's see how this works in a simple example.

You have a Total Market Opportunity of 150,000 prospects and based on your research, you divide them into groups with low, medium, and high priorities. Now, calculate the cost of sales and determine if the market has enough qualified prospects (see Fig. 3-3) If sales people randomly call on all prospects, they would have to make an average of over 72.3 sales calls for every sale. 150,000/ ((115,000 x 0.5%) + (25,000 x 2.0%) + (10,000 x 10.0%)) = 72.28. If however, the company only called on prospect with a high priority, it would have to only make 10 sales calls for every sale. The difference between 72.3 sales calls per sale and 10 sales calls per sale could mean the difference between profit and loss for a company.

Fig. 3-3

	Prospects per Segment	Sales Closing Rate/Segment	# Sales Calls Required/Sale
Total Prospects	150,000		
Low Priority Prospects	115,000	0.5%	200
Medium Priority Prospects	25,000	2.0%	50
High Priority Prospects	10,000	10.0%	10

The Map to the Market

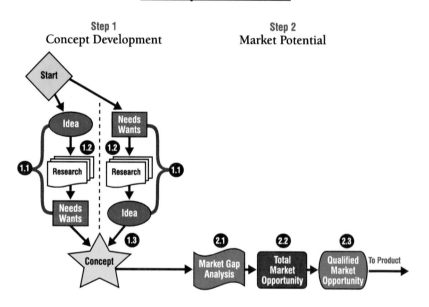

Step 1
Concept Development

Step 2
Market Potential

Step 1: Concept Development

1.1 Idea & Needs/Wants – Spark of Genius

As you see from the map, ideas can emerge from needs and wants in the marketplace or vice versa. The discussion over which came first is irrelevant. It doesn't really matter. New businesses are born from both ideas and needs/wants, but for the purpose of this section, we are going to show you the path that begins with the idea, goes through research, needs and wants validation, and then results in a concept. As you can see both paths use research and result in a concept.

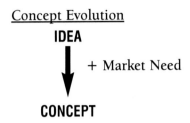

Concept Evolution

IDEA

+ Market Need

CONCEPT

If you came up with a great idea, you must do the research to determine whether there are needs and wants in the market for the product – based on priority, pain, and desire. Many entrepreneurs go wrong here because they begin with an idea and skip over asking the market what it thinks.

1.2 Research – Do Your Homework

Research is critical to answering the questions you're dying to know about your idea and the market. We're going to highlight a few research techniques that will help you better understand the market, but the fact is that you never really stop researching. Whether it's testing a product concept, marketing plan, or pricing strategy, research will constantly be an important asset.

The importance of research is a part of almost every topic in this chapter, so you'll see that we'll refer to it a number of times. Do not be misled and overwhelmed. We are not suggesting that there are multiple discrete research projects here, just that your initial research will be useful in many areas. When we talk about business research, there are really two different types with which to be familiar.

Primary Research

Research resulting from direct interaction with potential customers, primary research data comes out of focus groups, surveys, and one-on-one interviews. At the early stages of your business this type of data mining will be difficult because it's expensive and your idea might not be focused enough to ask the best questions. Therefore, you can use market proxies (i.e., a friend or family member who is in the target market) to ask basic questions and develop some insights.

Go Ahead, Ask Them... Survey Design

Surveys are part art, part science. On the art side, political pollsters are paid big money to finesse answers and get data that is favorable to one side over another. As you'll see, using one word differently in a question can completely change the corresponding answers that you'll get. For politicians, this is the goal, but if you're using your market research to make tough decisions about the business, you're probably going to want to ask questions honestly. Market research firms specialize in survey design and interpretation. These companies can perform the deep statistical analysis that would truly blow your mind in terms of the level of detail and precision you can learn about your targets. While certainly a market research firm is the way to go if you need this precision, it is expensive, and you can design a survey yourself if you just want to get a directional sense of the market's attitudes.

The types of questions typical in surveys at this point in your business are:
- Market: Who are you?
- Product/Service: What do you need/want?
- Pricing: How much are you willing to spend?
- Competition: Who else are you thinking about buying from?

Never ask a question that you could find the answer to somewhere else. It's a wasted question. If you feel there are other topics that are not included that relate to your business, add them too. Respondents, however, have a limited attention span for your survey. They might get bored, tired, or just impatient if you ask too many questions or the questions are too difficult to answer. You can "buy" more time from them if you offer an incentive for finishing, such as the possibility of a free trip or a $20 gift certificate. We have found that 20 questions which require no more than 5 minutes to complete is usually a good standard.

Surveys Must Be Easy to Use

We have a friend in corporate America whose company distributed a survey to all of its 5,000+ employees to get a sense of employee satisfaction. Only 30 responses came in. Why? The survey was a hassle to complete. Employees had to print out the survey, manually fill in their answers, and then finally, deliver their surveys to the person collecting them. The company had made it very difficult for the employees to comply. We recommend using an online survey company like Survey Monkey which, with a minimal monthly fee, allows you to create surveys online. Respondents just have to click on a link, which gets them into a professional-looking survey, fill it out and poof, that's it. You even get the results compiled for you in the form of nice little charts and graphs for your own analysis. The key is that your survey should be simple, well laid out, and easy to follow.

Wording Your Questions

At first pass, this may seem easy, but beware...

"Two priests, a Dominican and a Jesuit, are discussing whether it is a sin to smoke and pray at the same time. After failing to reach a conclusion, each goes off to consult his respective superior. The next week they meet again. The Dominican says, "Well, what did your superior say?" The Jesuit responded, "That's funny. My superior said it was a sin." Jesuit: "What did you ask him?" Reply: "I asked him if it was alright to smoke while praying." "Oh," says the Jesuit, "I asked my superior if it was alright to pray while smoking."[15]

Here are some of the common mistakes made in surveys.

→ **Double-barreled questions:** Do you believe that Jiffy Lube is the quickest and cheapest oil change? There are two questions in one and you won't know what respondents are really responding to.

→ **Overly vague questions:** How many members are there in your family? Does this refer to your immediate family or extended as well? You don't want respondents to have to think about the intent of the question before answering. The questions should be as clear as possible.

→ **Biased questions:** What did you dislike about the product? This forces respondents to come up with things they didn't like, when in fact, they might not have disliked anything. You should ask a general question – did you dislike anything about the product? If so, what?

→ **Loaded questions:** Do you think the US should allow public speeches against democracy? Do you think the US should forbid public speeches against democracy? These questions were actually tested and the results were amazing. 44% said "no" to the first question, and 28% said "yes" to the second.[16] Be careful how you phrase the questions if you're looking for unbiased answers.

---

[15] Pedhazur, Elazar. Measurement, design, and analysis: An Integrated Approach. New Jersey: Lawrence Erlbaum Associates, 1991.
[16] Biemer, Paul, Robert Groves, Lars Lyberg, Nancy Mathiowetz, and Seymour Sudman. Measurement Errors in Surveys. 1. Wiley-Interscience, 1991.

Structure of Survey

A typical survey follows an order and sequence of questions. Here's an example of a survey design about a new television set.

→ *Screening questions:* These questions are intended to identify target respondents. If you're asking about television preferences, you want to make sure respondents watch television.

→ *Warm-up questions:* These questions are intended to draw respondents in and show them that the survey is simple to complete. In the TV example, you can ask about how what brand they prefer, how much they watch, etc...

→ *Transition questions:* These questions are intended to gather information from respondents related to the meat of what you want to know. They require slightly more thought than the previous questions.

→ *Difficult questions:* These questions are intended to be the most difficult on the survey and require thought. Because they're toward the end of the survey and respondents can almost see the finish line, hopefully they'll keep going.

→ *Classifying questions:* These questions will help you segment the responses by demographics and psychographics.

Keeping Track

Surveys, at it turns out, can serve another function beyond telling you what the market thinks. Read the responses carefully. Those that are most enthusiastic about your concept and indicate a high priority for a solution are the ideal people to return to for Alpha testing (Chapter 4) and ultimately selling your final product. If participants are willing, collect their contact information and keep in touch with them. Your first customer will most likely emerge from this group.

"When implementing your survey, you should track the name of the company, title and person answering your questions, so you know who is best to call when you need good alpha test prospects."

Charlie

Secondary Research

If you are looking for more general market-related information, such as demographics (age, sex, income) or psychographics (buying preferences, lifestyle choices), you can often find relatively inexpensive sources of good compiled data.

Sources:

→ There are tens of thousands of industry associations in the U.S. – from the Association of Non-woven Fabrics Industry to the Tire Industry Association. By joining the industry association(s) most closely aligned with your target market/s, you can have access to a wealth of information that is very specific to your idea. For example, if you're opening up a new restaurant, the National Restaurant Association can provide real-time data and analysis of economic trends affecting the restaurant industry. In many cases, the annual cost of joining an industry association is relatively small (from a hundred dollars to a couple of thousand dollars a year).

→ Ask research librarians at the main branch of your city library or university for help. If you can give them very specific questions, they'll be able to direct you to the best sources. Despite the fact that everything is digitized and easier to use than it was even just a few years ago, due to the amount of information available, you need help to organize your search. Just as the right keyword web search can make all the difference in finding just what you want, enrolling the help of a librarian to focus your search can make a big difference in the results you get. While the cost of this is usually free or very minimal, we highly recommend that you provide them with a small gift and thank you note. This will go far if you need help in the future.

→ Purchase market specific information from databases. An example of this could be to purchase information (like mailing address, size of company, phone number, and title) of 1,000 random potential customers from InfoUSA. Likewise, credit related information from Equifax or Dun & Bradstreet can be helpful.

1.3 Concept – The Million Dollar Idea

We need to get really picky for a moment and carefully distinguish between an idea and a concept. An *idea* is a "pie in the sky" solution to problem. It has very little meat or substance to it. A *concept*, while still very basic, adds more substance and texture to this idea. For example, an idea is "developing a better way to access information on the world wide web." The concept, on the other hand, has evolved slightly, such as "creating a proprietary formula or algorithm to rank the relevancy of websites for web search queries and return those sites to the user." The concept comes out after you've begun to do some of the cursory research to put some meat on the bones of your idea. Your concept should have fuller dimension and be fleshed out a bit more than the idea. This will significantly help you to look at your product concept relative to what else is out there in the market.

Step 2: Market Potential

2.1 Market Gap Analysis – Find the Holes

One of the biggest mistakes entrepreneurs make is to assume that their concept is so revolutionary or so much better than anything else in the market that there is no competition. Let's face it, if there were no competitors in the world, it would be a whole lot easier to be successful…end of story. But the reality is that there are competitors both direct and indirect, and lots of them. In most cases successful competitors are taking potential customers and revenues away from you; therefore, it is critical to determine which ones are the biggest threats to your business and why.

A direct competitor is someone who does what you do. For example, if you own a bowling alley, your direct competitors would be all the bowling alleys in your area that might attract your customers. Indirect competitors are other types of entertainment businesses that your customers choose over a night of bowling, such as miniature golf, movies, and bars.

Since indirect competitors are vying for a slice of the total entertainment market, the more competitive you are, the more money will flow your way. Let's say you decide to add Karaoke in the evenings at the bowling alley to attract new customers. As a result, you receive an average of

50 additional customers every night. Most likely, you didn't woo these customers away from competing bowling alleys, but from your indirect competitors, like bars.

By broadening your market to include indirect competitors, you are more likely to think of more and better ways to attract customers. Just remember, if you think of yourself as a bowling alley, you're limiting your potential. If you see that you're actually in the entertainment business, you're expanding your potential.

2.2 Total Market Opportunity – How Big Is the Pie?
Remember,

$$\text{Total Qualified Prospects} =$$
$$\text{Total Market Opportunity x Qualification Factor}$$

Total Market Opportunity is anyone and everyone who has even the slightest chance of buying from your target market. It is the first preliminary prospect cut.

For example:

→ A developer in Denver, Colorado is interested in building houses that will sell for $1 million. The company estimates that they need to sell 100 houses over the next 3 years to make a sufficient profit to warrant going into this business. The developer wants to know if there are a sufficient number of potential customers in the market who can afford to buy these homes.

→ Their research shows that the average person buying a $1 million dollar house in Denver needs a minimum household income of $250,000 to qualify for a mortgage. The developer's research shows that according to the

Denver Chamber of Commerce, there are 17,000 households with an income of $250,000 or more.

→ Consequently, the total number of potential customers who can reasonably purchase a $1 million houses in Denver is 17,000.

The developer started her homework. On the other hand, many new companies mistakenly assume that anyone and everyone who shows even the slightest bit of interest in the product will be a customer. Not everyone is equally likely to buy, capable of buying, or easy to find. It's important to prioritize potential customers from most likely to buy to least likely to buy. To do this, our developer will have to drill down from all the potential customers in the universe that may buy to the number of potential customers with the requisite cash or credit, living in close proximity, with high enough needs, etc. Needless to say, the final number that represents your realistic market potential is usually much smaller than your initial estimation. The most effective (yet expensive) way is to develop and implement a statistically significant market survey. The key elements the developer would want to identify and measure are:

→ What specific prospect attributes relate to higher likelihood of purchase (Age, gender, demographics, finances...)?

→ What is the level of need or interest in your product (broken down by target market)?

→ What percentage of each potential target market is likely to buy within the next 3-6 months?

→ How much value does the average prospect believe they can derive from your product in the first year post-purchase?

→ What do they expect the product to cost and what are they willing to pay?

→ How do the different target markets perceive your product next to competitors?

If you don't have the expertise or the funds to spend to develop this type of research, you can develop your own market rankings analysis. This exercise helps you stack up the different possible markets against each other based on factors that you've deemed are important in order to distinguish the markets with the greatest potential from those less lucrative. Here's how to do it:

First, build a matrix. The matrix will have the number of columns equal to the number of target markets you're evaluating, plus one. For our example, the target prospects are companies with different annual revenues from $250,000 to $10 million. If you're comparing seven target markets, you would develop a matrix that has eight columns and ten rows. The first column will be the list of the eight factor questions presented below, the remaining seven columns will include each of the target markets you're comparing.

Now add eight rows. We found that the following eight target market factors are best to rank each of your potential target markets.

1. How much benefit does the average prospect in that target market reap in their first year by using your product?
2. What is the priority of your product/service to overall business success/profitability?
3. What is the likelihood of the average prospect having a sufficient budget available for your product?
4. What kind of connections do you have? What is your ability to get in front of each prospective market?

5. How deeply entrenched is your potential competition within each target market?
6. What is the level of the decision-maker within a company who will ultimately decide to buy or not buy your product? (the higher the level, the higher the ranking score)
7. How difficult and costly is it to get market specific leads such as mailing lists, access to publications, trade show participant lists, etc.?
8. What is the relative size of each market; i.e., number of potential customers? (the larger the number, the higher the ranking score)

Now, for each potential target market, rank on a scale of 1 – 10 each factor (with 10 being the highest ranking and 1 being the lowest). While this is subjective, it will give you valuable directional information. Once you have determined a score for each potential target market factor, add up each column score to get the total score for each. The target market with the highest score would be your company's primary target market and this is the market you should be spending the overwhelming majority of your time and on which to spend marketing and sales dollars.

Fig. 3-4

Target Markets Revenues:	$250,000	$250k-$1M	$1M-$2.5M	$2.5M-$5M	$5M-$10M	>$10M
Factor 1:	6	3	8	6	7	4
Factor 2:	8	2	6	3	5	5
Factor 3:	5	6	9	4	6	7
Factor 4:	6	5	8	5	8	9
Factor 5:	4	2	7	3	4	6
Factor 6:	8	5	9	5	8	9
Factor 7:	7	6	10	5	5	7
Factor 8:	7	6	8	6	5	7
Total Score	51	35	65	37	48	54
Rank Highest to Lowest:	3	6	1	5	4	2

In doing this analysis for your specific business, you may need to customize the eight factors for your industry/idea.

2.3 Qualification Factor – Reality Check

After you've gotten a sense of the total market opportunity and determined which target markets look the most desirable, it's time to drill down on your projection of how many customers will actually buy. The Total Market Opportunity is not a good basis for how many products you'll actually sell. There are a variety of factors that diminish the market potential.

Going back to the previous example of the home building company, the factors that reduce the number of buyers are those:

→ Not interested in where the developer is building
→ Don't like the style of homes offered
→ Would prefer a used home

→ Don't want to spend $1 million on a house
→ Not looking to move

Therefore, the developer must estimate and discount the total market opportunity by the percentage of potential customers who fit into these categories. This is the Qualification Factor.

Here research plays an important role again. In her survey, the developer should add the following questions:

→ Would you be interested in purchasing a $1 million dollar or more expensive house in the next 3 years?
→ Would you consider purchasing a house in the specific area of Denver mentioned?
→ Would you consider buying a particular style home?
→ When looking for your next home, would you be more interested in purchasing a new home or a used home?

Conclusion

Throughout this section, we've helped you to confirm or disprove that there is a large enough number of qualified potential customers with high priority needs and/or wants to justify building your business. You also have determined that you have a concept for which you can build a product that will satisfy these needs and wants – better than any competitor. This was important pre-thinking that will ultimately make the next step, building the product, so much more successful.

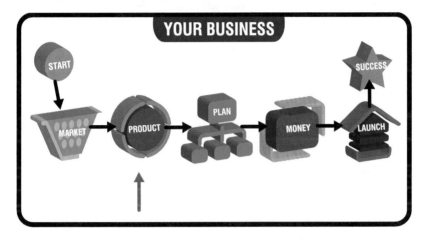

"Quality in a product or service is not what the supplier puts in.
It is what the customer gets out and is willing to pay for."

- Peter F. Drucker, Writer and Management Guru

"The true creator is necessity,
who is the mother of invention."

- Plato, Ancient Greek Philosopher

Objective

To show you how to turn your concept into an attractive, functioning product that delivers high priority benefits and substantial value for your prospects with a sufficient profit for the company.

What You Need to Know About the Product

We're going to guide you through the steps required to build successful products. Remember from the last chapter, when we refer to products we're actually talking about the full range of products and services that you could possibly create. We will now help you turn your concept into a viable, successful, and profitable product. This requires you to ask a lot of questions, and then tinker with the product to get it just right. Rarely does the final product look exactly like your initial concept.

Features, Benefits, and Fast Cars

Contrary to what many entrepreneurs believe there are significant differences between a product's benefits and features.

Benefits are the underlying advantages of your product that a customer is buying. While they might not necessarily be what are advertised "on the box," benefits are the real reason why people buy. What is tricky for the entrepreneur is that different people may derive different benefits from the same product. For example, to me, this new red Lamborghini is the sleekest car on the road and that is my reason for buying. For you, however, the red Lamborghini is the fastest car on the block and that is the reason you spent a quarter of a million bucks. One of us likes looks and one of us likes speed, so we each derive different – and equally valid – benefits from the car. Your challenge is to communicate your product's benefits as widely and clearly as possible, to the broadest market you can.

Features on the other hand, are the product traits that are written "on the box." For example, the Lamborghini has a 6 liter V12 engine, a sunroof, and a discount with a local bail bondsman to get you out of jail when you're arrested for driving at MACH 1. Here's the key: These features are the means by which customers derive benefits. They do not possess any value on their own; it is the connection that consumers make to the benefits that is critical. If we are the only customers buying the car and we only care about either speed or appearance, there is no reason why the makers of Lamborghini would ever add a fuel efficient engine because that benefit might not be important to us. To appease us, Lamborghini would only have to make the car sleeker or faster. Now, in reality, people invariably derive more than one benefit from their purchases, but they rank those benefits from most important to least important. Leather seats, a feature offered to customers at a premium price, have both quantitative benefits (durability, ease of cleaning) and qualitative benefits (image, status). Depending on how prospects weigh the importance of each of these benefits will determine whether or not they buy.

Charlie

"My students, always trying to show me up, say something like this, 'Charlie, wait a minute, what about a rear deck spoiler on a car? It's clearly a feature on a car, but doesn't have any benefit unless you're driving 150 mph.' True indeed, but assuming you are going to drive near the speed limit, the spoiler adds value because it conveys a fashionable, cool image -- and that image is the benefit that drivers are buying."

Your Perception is My Reality

Benefits are both objective and subjective, based on individual tastes and preferences. This means that the same product can offer benefits to one customer and nothing positive to another (and possibly even detriments). Who is right? Well, they both are. They just have different perspectives.

When talking about a product, the same difference in perspectives is common. What's really important is not that they're both correct but why they differ, how much they differ, and what that really means for the company. The typical reasons for these differences between the customer's reality and company's perception are:

1. Prospects are often skeptical about being able to obtain and enjoy the benefits that companies promote for their products.

2. Prospects don't pay attention to all the benefits a product delivers because there are often too many benefits being promoted at once.

3. Prospects believe that they are different from other prospects and therefore don't believe they will be able to obtain the same degree of benefits as other prospects.

In many cases, a prospect's perception of a product's value is *less than half* of what the entrepreneur believes it to be. This striking dichotomy makes the product seem much less valuable in the eyes of the prospect and, consequently, more difficult for the company to sell. Sadly, many first-time entrepreneurs miss this point – they assume that because they see the benefits of their product, prospects will see them too. At the end of the day, prospect perception is the only reality that matters. Later in this chapter, we will show you how successful entrepreneurs take this into account and what they do to minimize prospects' discounted perceptions.

Who's Buying?

Here's one more wrinkle. Hopefully you accept that the fact that the customer's perception is what really matters. But who is really your customer? Often entrepreneurs confuse end users with buyers. Sure they can be one of the same, but often times they are two different entities (or people) with two different perspectives, developing your product only for the end user without considering who really makes the buying decision, is shortsighted and can cost you dearly in the end. Here's how it happens: You will be building your product for a specific user, and as such, you'll want to know how that user perceives your product. At that time, this person's perception is the most important, but don't assume that it's the only one that matters. Others may have more influence on, or may actually make the final decision. For example, there may be C-level executives, managers or other buyers at the prospective customer – who might not even directly use your product – involved in the decision. You have to figure out how to provide enough value to both the decision-maker as well as the user to ensure that your product is purchased.

Here is a quick example. You company is trying to sell a $300,000 customer service software package to a Fortune 500 company that will save the company over $1 million in the first three years. You make the presentation to the VP of Customer Service and she loves the product. As your salesperson walks out the door, he is confident that he just made the sale. But there's a catch. The CFO will have to sign off on the purchase because of its cost; however, because of other significant capital expenditures the company is making, the CFO is concerned about the negative cash flow associated with the purchase. So even if the VP loved the product and promotes it, the CFO still might reject it. Had the entrepreneur known that the CFO was integral in the decision-making process, he might have made sure that the CFO was invited to the sales presentation and developed strategies to minimize the CFO's concerns.

You've seen how perceptions and reality work and whose perceptions really can count. So now we turn to the object of those perceptions: **Value.**

It's All About Value

By now you have probably noticed that we use the term value quite often. We introduced the concept in Chapter 3 as a variable in the sales probability equation:

Product Attractiveness = Priority x Value x Communication

Remember that we explained the importance of priority as the first determinant in analyzing whether anyone will buy your product. As a ranking of prospects' needs and/or wants and as a measurement of the importance of satisfying a given problem or desire, priority is the qualifier that determines whether your product even makes it onto the prospect's radar. Without a high enough priority, regardless of how many bells and whistles your product has (or how much value you provide), prospects just won't care, and apathy is your biggest enemy. Yet once prospects decide, however, that they have a high enough priority need or want, then (and only then) will they investigate the various options. While priority drives the decision to buy, value is how prospects compare competitive product alternatives and make their purchase decision.

Analyzing value helps prospects compare products and make choices. Naturally, solutions that offer more value have the greatest likelihood of being purchased. We also explained in Chapter 3 that value is the relationship between a product's benefits and costs. A product delivers value when its benefits outweigh its costs. While this all might seem obvious in theory, most first time entrepreneurs muck it up. They don't truly understand the importance of value nor do they really know how to measure it. If you accept the proposition that there is a clear relationship between the value a product provides and its likelihood of being purchased, then it should also be clear that when a customer compares two products side-by-side that address the same priority, the likelihood of purchase will be determined by the relative value that each provides.

Fig. 4-1 illustrates this relationship. Of course more value leads to a greater likelihood of purchase, but the connection is not linear. As value rises, the likelihood of purchase doesn't increase as quickly. To increase a product's value, a company must invest more in the product – which leads to higher product costs or lower prices. You have to find the sweet spot between over-investing and under-investing that will get enough prospects up and buying.

Fig. 4-1

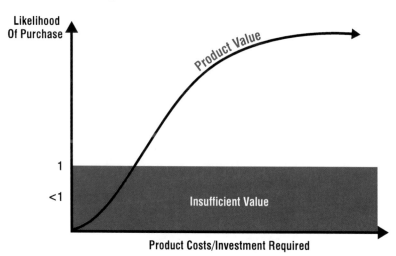

Product Value and Its Impact On Prospect Purchase and Product Costs

Most entrepreneurs (and companies) look at value very narrowly. Typically, they use the same equation that has been used for decades:

$$\text{Product Value} \quad = \quad \frac{\text{Benefits}}{\text{Purchase Costs}}$$

The product value equation is sometimes referred to as the value proposition. The formula is very simple. When benefits equal costs, product value equals one. Product value is greater than one when the benefits are greater than the price. In reality, however, this equation does not fully explain how prospects determine value because the equation only considers quantitative factors.

Quantitative factors are relatively easy to measure and can usually be denominated in dollars or time. Quantitative factors that enhance value are called benefits; those that subtract value are called costs.

Qualitative factors are a bit trickier. These are not easy to measure and are driven by both emotions and inertia. Although they're more ambiguous or fuzzy, they are no less important. In fact, in many cases they can have much more of an impact on a prospect's decision making process than their quantitative siblings. Just like quantitative factors can be either benefits or costs, so too can qualitative factors. The latter takes into account the intrinsic costs and benefits associated with human emotions and inertia to determine value. So, in the context of business, what exactly are emotions and inertia?

> **Emotions** play a critical role in all our lives and in how prospects make purchase decisions. Seldom does anyone make a decision solely based on facts or hard data. Despite best intentions, emotions get in the way – for better or for worse. As you can well imagine, they have either a positive or negative impact on a product. Take a moment and look at your watch. Why did you choose this one? If the only purpose of your watch was to tell time, would you still have selected this watch? Your choice of watches was most likely influenced by positive emotional factors such as looking and feeling good or exuding a certain image, or features such as an alarm or stopwatch. Every buyer might have their own reasons that transcend a common price versus benefits analysis.

While positive emotions can pave the way to a sale, negative feelings about a product can kill any deal no matter how much perceived quantitative value the company believes it offers. Some of the more influential negative emotions in the decision process include risk, fear, anxiety, curiosity, etc. If you heard that the watch company was involved in shady dealings or unlawful activity and these things are very important to you, it will not matter how much real value the watch provides.

But it is even more complicated than that because emotions cut both ways. Fear, for example, can be a very effective tool in influencing priorities. If prospects have an ever-rising fear of the consequences of a certain problem, their priority to find a solution rises. Some companies base their entire selling strategy on leveraging this fear. Just think about the home security companies that harness the fear of a break-in by showing images of frightened families and stolen possessions. However, fear can also act as a deterrent to purchasing. If prospects perceive more risk by buying a product, their likelihood of purchase will decrease.

Positive emotions are considered benefits and add value to a product, while negative emotions are considered costs and reduce value. For example, let's say that you are a manager at a small computer company interested in buying a mainframe computer server. While XYZ Computing might offer a quantifiably better product for a lower price than IBM, XYZ is an unknown company. If you chose XYZ's product and it works, you're only doing your job. If the server does-n't work, you could be blamed for choosing an unknown supplier and lose your job. If you choose IBM's product, however-er, and it doesn't work, you're much less likely to be blamed because everyone assumes that IBM's products always work. Your fear of potentially losing your job is a negative emotional factor that decreases the value of XYZ's server relative to IBM's.

Since the traditional value equation doesn't account for emotions, this equation would predict XYZ's server provided more value and would be more likely to be purchased. Depending on the level of fear, this may or may not be the case. Most likely, while IBM doesn't provide as much quantifiable value in this example, the notion that you will sleep easier at night knowing that you went with a top-notch company over an unknown brand compensates for the extra cost. This is of course, where the famous saying "No one gets fired for buying IBM".

Inertia, a concept borrowed from physics, explains why an object will remain at rest unless acted upon by an outside force. In business, inertia works like this: People are naturally resistant to change, and often buying new products requires people to alter their behavior.

Even if your product is better and will save them time or money, there is still resistance to overcome; your prospects need a push. The more effort required of prospects to purchase, learn, use, or dispose of a product, the less likely they are going to buy. A product's related inertia reduces value. And while emotions can be used to positively impact a prospect's purchase decision, inertia almost always has a negative impact on a prospect's purchase decisions.

To bring this all together, we have developed the following diagram:

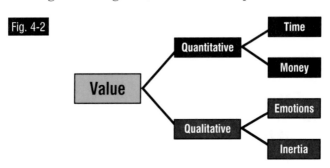

Fig. 4-2

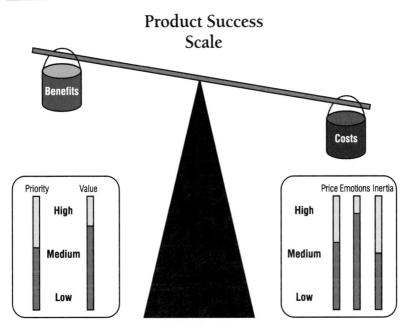

One goal in meeting with prospects early on in the product development stage is to identify both quantitative and qualitative factors and determine how much they impact your product's value. Often entrepreneurs are blinded by love. They're so in love with their product that they fail to see its weaknesses. Prospects, however, will help you see the light. One prospect might tell you that your product is too difficult to use. Another might say that it requires too much effort to learn how to use it. And another might say that they fear your product won't work well. It's important to hear all the different possible issues that might dissuade prospects from buying – especially before you've fully built the product. While certainly not a statistically significant finding, these conversations give you a directional sense of what prospects are thinking and where potential issues may arise.

Let's see how all of this worked in one of our companies.

In 2003, we launched a company called MedBuddy, an Internet-based physician-to-patient communication tool designed for primary care practices. This online tool gave patients and physicians round-the-clock access to each other for non-emergency requests. It also gave physicians their first automated connection to patient's health insurance companies, pharmacies, and specialists. The MedBuddy system consisted of 11 unique online applications:

Fig. 4-4

MedBuddy
Product Features

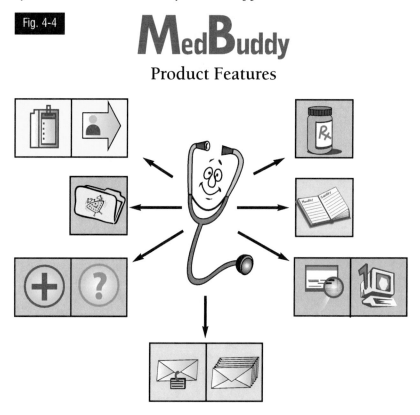

From re-filling a prescription to booking an appointment, MedBuddy enabled patients to interact with medical professionals via the Internet without even picking up the phone. The benefits for physicians and their staff were numerous, including:

→ **Time:** The tool saves physicians, nurses, and staff time through online prescription refills, insurance verification; appointment scheduling, answering frequently asked questions, and transmitting test results. MedBuddy enables each of the aforementioned routine tasks, which were done over the phone, to now be completed online and through e-mail. The average amount of time saved per month per physician is 32.5 minutes, per nurse 85 minutes, and per staff member 127.5 minutes which corresponds to a total savings of $3,097.30 per month.

→ **Incremental Income:** "Online visits" are an entirely new source of revenues for physicians via MedBuddy. Requiring just a few minutes at their own convenience, physicians can review a patient's health issues or questions through the system and respond with medical advice, suggestions for treatment, or next steps. The fee for this service is $30.00 per visit and over 70% of the time, the patient does not have to come into the office at all. This saves patients some hassle while enabling them to receive a more thorough medical evaluation than possible by phone. Additionally, MedBuddy's automated reminders reduce the number of appointments missed by patients, which enhances patient care and increases physician income. On average, MedBuddy conservatively generated $1,800.00 from online visits and a reduction in appointment "no shows" per month.

→ Combining these two sets of benefits, MedBuddy delivers a total incremental value of $4,897.30 per month $3,097.30 (time savings) + $1,800.00 (incremental revenue). Using an average cost per physician a month of $350.00 for the MedBuddy system, the projected value of MedBuddy (using the value proposition formula above) equals 13.99.

$$\text{Value Proposition} = \$4{,}897.30 \, / \, \$350.00 = 13.99$$

For the record, very few products deliver value anywhere near 14 times cost. As such, MedBuddy should have been a very attractive product to physicians. This, however, did not prove to be the case. Our conservative projections fell short by over 50%. Given that MedBuddy provided such high value, the obvious question is: why wasn't it a major success? Why weren't physicians knocking down our door? Here's what we found:

Emotions-based factors:
- → Concern that patients might not like the product, which would lead to attrition
- → Fear of physicians, nurses, and staff appearing incompetent by being unable to learn or use the product
- → Fear that nurses and staff would have to put in additional hours to respond to patient requests
- → Concern that the product would not work effectively and that patient information will get lost
- → Fear that our company, which was new, would not be around to trouble shoot and fix problems

Inertia-based factors:
- → Getting staff to change the way they currently interacted with patients and buy into a new process
- → Spending their limited time to learn a new product

With this assortment of seemingly random qualitative factors that could impact product value, how do you know what's really important and how these factors stack up against each other? We just told you that one of the major differences between quantitative and qualitative factors is that the latter aren't easily measurable. After all, there's no emotional measuring stick. However, you can and should measure the *relative importance* of the various emotional factors. In other words, you can determine how important one emotional factor is when compared to another. The most important factors are those which require the most attention.

Earlier, we discussed the importance of asking the market questions and going through the due diligence in your research to best meet your market's requirements. In order to rank each of the issues that could potentially do the most damage to your product, include them in your survey and ask your potential customers what they think.

This won't necessarily be the most precise indicator, but it should tell you what the biggest issues are. The issues that rank higher have a greater impact on the product's value.

Most likely, you're not going to be able to solve each and every one of these issues, but understanding what the biggest issues are helps you to prioritize what benefits or features you need to add to the product to make it more sellable – and effectively minimize prospects' concerns.

For MedBuddy, we found that the following three issues were most important to the physicians we surveyed:

→ They believed that it would be very difficult to get their staff to buy-in to the product because they were already so busy.

→ They were concerned that our company wouldn't be around long-term to support the product and trouble-shoot.

→ They believed it would be difficult to get their partners to agree to buy the product.

These factors effectively chipped away at the relative value of the product and posed a serious challenge to our company. These hang-ups also oriented us as to where we needed to tweak the product – its benefits and features – in order to overcome these concerns.

For example, because "staff buy-in" came out as the most significant issue preventing purchase of MedBuddy, allaying this concern was our top priority. To encourage use, we created an easy to use, interactive flash presentation that explained how to use MedBuddy in just 10 minutes. In the next section (building strategy, tactics, and execution), we will show what other levers you can use to dispel concern and motivate purchase of your product, but it's best to begin by looking at the product itself to determine where value could be created.

Despite our best efforts to minimize MedBuddy's pain points, we were unable to overcome one surprising thing. It seemed that the partners in medical groups didn't trust each other's business decisions. It was almost as if when one partner liked a proposal, another partner would veto it. So, it really didn't matter what MedBuddy did. Since this market wasn't working we turned our attention to health service departments at colleges and universities. Through our research, we found that student health services were run by one physician – and therefore circumvented a need to get buy-in for the product from a number of partners. Additionally, we found that staff isn't nearly as busy and had more time for learning a new product. Within six months of reorienting to this market, MedBuddy was up and running in eight student health centers around the country.

The Nexus of Priority and Value

There is an important relationship between the priority level that a product addresses and the value it provides. While of course value still must be greater than cost if it's to have any chance with consumers, the higher the prospect's priority for a solution, the less value the product needs to provide in order to be acceptable.

By overlaying the value graph with the priority graph from chapter 3 you will be able to see how priority and value both impact the probability for making a sale (Fig. 4-5).

Fig. 4-5

Where Does Your Product Fall?

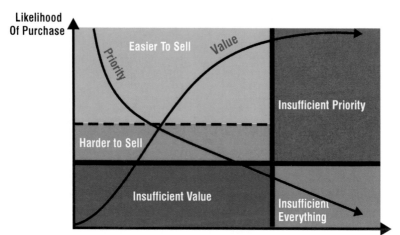

By way of example:

On a hot summer day, you and your friends are playing soccer two hours from home and in the middle of nowhere. You've consumed all of the drinks you brought by the end of the first half of the game and by the end of the game, you are exhausted and your throat is parched. To satisfy that thirst immediately, the only option open is a local bar. This place only sells beer, but there's no brand or price mentioned on the menu. When the bartender comes over to take your order, the group virtually asks in unison, "How much?" The clever bartender sees an opportunity. Everyone is extremely thirsty and he can smell a profit. He tells everyone the beer costs $10.00/glass, which is of course ridiculously expensive given that you can get a beer anywhere else for $3.00/glass. But you're not anywhere else. You're here, in the middle of nowhere and two hours from home. Since you are all so thirsty and assuming everyone has more than enough money, would you buy?

When we posed this question to our students, respondents almost universally said "yes." Your high priority (satisfying thirst) made a low-value product much more valuable. After finishing your glass, you are all feeling a little better but realize you are still thirsty. And again, the bartender swoops in. He instinctively knows that you're no longer as desperate as before and you're not likely to pay the same $10.00 for another glass, but he knows that you are still likely to pay more than the $3.00 he usually charges. He tells you, "It's your lucky day, we're having a special, and the second beer is half price, only $5.00." So would you buy the second beer?

Again the overwhelming majority of our students said "yes," they'd buy. After the second beer, the bartender realizes the value of an additional beer has decreased, and that you're not likely to spend $5.00 for another beer. This time, he tells you about his bar's three beers special. The third beer is only $3.00/glass, which is the same price you would pay if you went elsewhere for beer. Again, more than half of our students say they would buy the third beer.

After finishing three beers, the bartender realizes that everyone is pretty much satiated, but he can't resist the opportunity to make another buck. He offers you the fourth beer for $2.00 (still giving him an additional $1.00 profit per glass). Realizing that this was a good deal, and cheaper than you can get anywhere else, would you buy another beer?

We found that just less than half of those we polled would indeed purchase the fourth beer. After the fourth beer, most say they've had about all they can handle. The bartender, still aching to make every penny he can off of you, offers the fifth beer for $1.25 each, a virtual steal anywhere else. Would you buy it? As you probably guessed, less than a quarter of respondents said they would. Even though this was an attractive deal, the actual value of another beer would be minimal or possibly even negative (one more beer could make you sick). Consequently, the same beer that had a value of $10.00 less than an hour earlier no longer provides even $1.25 worth of value.

In this story, as in real life, the value that people associate with a product is directly tied to their level of priority. The higher a prospect's priority is for a solution, the more valuable the solution is to the prospect. The more valuable the solution is, the higher the price the prospect is willing to pay. Consequently, product value is tied in some way to prospect priority. In addition, *to a much smaller degree* value can also influence priority but only to a point (as you can see by the fourth and fifth beer examples above). So in a world without competition, product value is directly tied to priority.

However, in the real world, there is competition - usually lots of it. Competitive products effectively put a floor on the minimum amount of value a product can offer in order to still be attractive to prospects. Our beer-chugging soccer players would not have paid $10.00 for the first beer if they could have gone across the street and bought it for $3.00. Consequently, value is also a function of competition. And yes, life is too short for mediocre beer.

Innovation, Emotion, Opportunity… And Luggage

Before we move into the step-by-step analysis of building products, let's review a few things:

→ Products that deliver greater value are of course easier to sell than products that offer less value (given equal priority levels).

→ The more familiar a prospect is with a product, the more comfortable they will be to purchase it.

→ Value is heavily influenced by both quantitative and qualitative factors, and of those qualitative factors, risk and fear typically tend to dominate because people are afraid of the unknown.

There is one more thing you need to consider as you pursue a product idea. Entrepreneurs need to categorize their product, in general terms, as being either high innovation or low innovation. Not only will this have a serious impact on the value and purchase decision, but it can also affect your costs. Really, it can. Here's why:

Low innovation products are new products that are just slight variations of existing products. While these products are different from what's out there in the market already, there is some familiarity with the product. As a result, prospects tend to be less fearful of buying. This translates into a lower cost of sale for the entrepreneurial venture. Low innovation products offer additional benefits or a specifically-customized set of benefits to meet a specific market niche's requirements. For example, Apple didn't create the first MP3 player, they just made it easier to use and better looking with the iPod. Toyota didn't invent the car; they just made it more reliable. Jiffy Lube didn't invent the oil change; they just delivered the service quicker and more conveniently for customers. Low innovation products are a lower risk way to build a successful new business.

High innovation products are new to the marketplace and not closely related to any other products. The risk associated with the purchase is likely to be correlated with higher anxiety and greater emotional costs. To offset these costs, highly innovative products must offer substantially greater benefits. By being harder to sell, these products will likely create a major cash issue: To allay the fears of your prospects, you will need to make a much greater investment in marketing and sales than if you were selling a low innovation product. Since most new ventures and small businesses don't have a lot of cash, coming up with the funds to ramp up marketing and sales efforts is difficult.

While we are certainly not saying that you can't be successful with high innovation products, they require substantially more investment dollars and longer time frames to become profitable when compared to their low innovation products counterparts. The innovation level is something to be considered paramount when developing financial projections, a process which we will handle in Chapter 6.

While high innovation products usually generate the most excitement, draw the most attention, and create the perception that only they offer big opportunities to entrepreneurs, don't fall into the trap of believing that this is the only way for entrepreneurs to success. Low innovation products can deliver huge opportunities. Here is an example:

Q: How long has the wheel been around in human society?

A: Let's say for thousands of years to be conservative.

Q: How long has luggage been around?

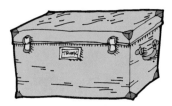

A: Documentation exists that the Holy Roman Empire utilized some form a luggage. So let's say that luggage has been around for at least 2,000 years.

Q: So when did someone come up and patent luggage with wheels?

A: Bernard Sadow, CEO of U.S. Luggage, developed the prototype of luggage on wheels in 1972. The idea was ridiculed and rejected by a buyer at Macy's, but two weeks later Mr. Sadow met with a Macy's executive who loved the idea. And thus began rolling luggage. Even though wheels on luggage seems like an obvious solution, this low innovation product made Sadow millions.[17]

And lest you thought that wheeled luggage marked the end of suitcase-based innovation, think again:

"In case style and craftsmanship weren't enough to lure in suitcase shoppers, customers who purchase luggage from Carpisa stores in Italy during a special year-long promotion get an unusual perk – insurance for their bags against any loss by any airline worldwide."[18] This innovative partnership between a luggage manufacturer and

---

[17] Kilgannon, Corey. "From Suitcases on Wheels to Tear-Free Onion Slicers." New York Times 06 Aug 2000, natl. ed.

[18] http://www.springwise.com/index_tourism_travel.xml

financial services firm offers a unique benefit that increases the value of the product to consumers. Who knew?

The Map to the Product

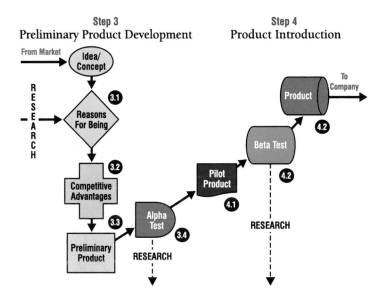

Step 3: Preliminary Product Development

3.1 Reason for Being – Standing Out From the Crowd

Turning your concept into a product begins not with a hammer and nails, but with knowing your reason for being. Based on what you learned earlier in this chapter, you need to answer these questions:

→ What makes your product different, unique, or special from the rest of what's out there?

→ What benefits are you going to offer your prospects that they either can't get today or that you can deliver better than your competitors can?

→ What is the value you will deliver and how well does it compare to the cost of buying the product?

The Dogfish Head Brewery, a beer manufacturer in Delaware, literally puts its reason for being – experimental or "extreme" beers – on the bottle. Dogfish Head uses non-standard beer ingredients, such as green raisins and beet sugar in their Raison D'Être beer line. The beer was rated as "American Beer of the Year" in January 2000 by Malt Advocate Magazine.

Wal-Mart, the world's largest retailer, decided that its reason for being was to offer the lowest priced products in the market. At the time Wal-Mart, Kmart, Target, and the other major retailers basically offered the same products, so there was little differentiation between them. Wal-Mart, however, changed the game and built a company around "everyday low prices" by purchasing product in larger volume at lower prices than their competitors, which they then passed through to customers.

So what is your product's raison d'être? Be very precise in your answer or you're likely to "me too" your product into irrelevance. What the world does not need is another product that doesn't do anything different or better than products that already exist for the same price. As we said earlier in this chapter, don't be misled into thinking that you have to give the world something it has never seen before (i.e., a high innovation product). While this would be great, it's not realistic for every product in every category in every market. Assuming for a moment that you don't have that one-in-a-million concept, what is it that you will provide that will urge your prospects to reach into their tight little wallets and pulled out their hard earned cash? That's your reason for being.

For this to have any meaning or impact on your prospects, you must be able to communicate it. In fact, we believe that you must be able to explain why your prospect should buy your product in 20 words or less to be effective. *That's right, 20 words or less.* If it takes more than 20 words, then you're not focusing enough and will probably lose your prospect's attention. You've got to hook them with your reason for being. Then you must be able to explain each benefit of your product as precisely as possible; the more detailed you are, the better. For example, saying you're going to "provide better service" is much too general and, therefore, of little value. Instead you need to explain:

→ Why better service is important to your prospects
→ How you define better service
→ What exactly you're going to be doing differently from your competitors in order to deliver this better service
→ How you and your prospects will measure it
→ How your prospects will benefit from getting better service
→ What you can provide that a sufficiently large group of prospects really want and can't get anywhere else and that you can do better and so others can't easily copy

Let's see how you would actually determine your reason for being. Let's say that your new company has developed a new formula for house paint called Eternity's Best House Paint. Your R&D department told you that your product will differ from competitors along various important dimensions – from number of coats required to durability to cost (Fig. 4-6).

But what's really important to prospects? Again remember back to the market survey. You should have a sense of this already and be able to rank order the benefits from most important to least important. Put an asterisk next to each benefit that you're considering including in your product that competition does not offer. Put a check next to each benefit that you plan to offer that your competitor's product also offers. Finally, list all competitors' product benefits that you're not planning on including in your product. Refer to Fig. 4-7 to see how Eternity's Best would do this:

Fig. 4-6

	Eternity's Best House Paint	Competitors
# of coats of paint required/ job	One coat of paint	Two coats for light colors and three coats for darker colors
Product durability	Guaranteed not to chip, fade or discolor for 100 years	At most 5-10 year guarantees
Paint as home insulation	Provides an added insulation value of R-10; this will save the average house owner 5% on their annual heating and air conditioning bills, which translates to $125 for the average customers	Very few exterior or interior paints even market insulation benefits, and those that do offer much less than Eternity's Best House Paint
Product costs (avg. house requires 40 gal.)	$70/ gallon	$35/ gallon
Labor costs	$50, watching a 30 minute video, answering 10 questions to be certified as Eternity's Best house painter and qualify for product guarantee	None

Fig. 4-7

	Eternity's Best Benefits		Competitor's Benefits	
	Better coverage	✔	Faster application time	
*	Longer lasting		Wider selection of colors	
*	Insulating properties		Tie in with other products (like brushes)	
*	Labor cost		Product cost	
	Environmentally friendly	✔		
*	Long warranty	✔		

Now look at your lists. How many benefits does your product offer that your competitors' products don't? Do you believe they would be highly valued by your prospects?

Your reason for being should relate to a highly-valued benefit that you offer that the competition does not. In this case, Eternity's Best should clearly trump the fact that its paint lasts longer and insulates better. Obviously, they've begun to do this with the name of the company and product alone.

Michael

"A Note of Caution: When developing your product, it's important that you consider not only what you're going to do better, but what you can do to protect your company from competitors copying it. These are called barriers to entry and we'll have a lot more to say about these in a minute...."

3.2 Competitive Advantages – It's Time to Take Advantage

Whatever you've determined as your reason for being, you now have to make sure that you can deliver on it better than your competitors. It's one thing to say that you're going to offer the lowest prices, but without a real cost-efficient advantage over your competitors, they are likely to respond quickly and undercut you, killing your reason for being. If, however, you have a real and defensible advantage over your competition, then you have something worthwhile.

Competitive advantages are essential for building a successful business and are often the company's reason for being. Competitive advantages stand in relation to both the needs and wants of the market and to what competitors already deliver. They are built on the back of the company's strengths. If, for example, a company has exclusive access to unique components, materials, expertise or technologies that it can exploit, it should be able to offer greater product value than its competition. In the case of Eternity's Best, these advantages included the insulating quality and durability because let's face it: eternity is a long time.

But the existence of competitive advantages will not guarantee success; they only serve to increase the *likelihood* of it. It is not unusual to see companies that have a competitive advantage fail to use or exploit them effectively. To be successful, a company still must capitalize on its competitive advantages.

Offense, Defense, and Sustainable Advantages

While competitive advantages are the building blocks of a successful new venture, you should think of them more as an offensive instrument. Their primary purpose is to enhance customer value; this in turn positively differentiates your company from its competitors. And – we can't say it enough – the greater the relative value delivered, the greater the chances are for a product or service sale. When you have competitive advantages that are really strong, you can keep competitors out of the market, and in this case the competitive advantages are called "barriers to entry".

However, as sports fans know, a strong offense does not guarantee success. You also need a strong defense. Why? Even if you have strong competitive advantages, any weaknesses you have will likely be exploited by competitors. So to keep a competitor from exploiting weaknesses, you need to address them with strong competitive advantages known as "sustainable" competitive advantages. For Eternity's Best, the competitive advantages that act as barriers to entry are paint coverage and the durability guarantee. This is especially true because the company has a patent on the ingredients that gives the paint its 100 year durability. The company, however, does not have the patent on the technology that gives the paint its insulating qualities. Even though the paint offers better insulation now and is a competitive advantage to other paints, it is not sustainable because others can copy and exploit this technology.

It is not uncommon to hear barriers to entry described as "high" or "low". A patent gives your company a high barrier to entry. A simple head start, however, is a low barrier to entry because the short-term advantage you gain from being first probably won't do much to deter competitors from getting in the game.

We Don't Have No Stinking Weaknesses

Identifying weaknesses is a difficult task, not only for new ventures but for more mature ventures as well. There are a number of reasons for this. Entrepreneurs steering their new companies are inclined to be overwhelmingly optimistic and often ignore or minimize the significance of weaknesses. For larger firms, senior management must encourage their staff, to honestly present company weaknesses if they even want to get a real picture of issues plaguing the firm. Lower level employees, who are at the front lines of the business, are often aware of issues but don't want to be the one responsible for conveying the information to senior management. Even though this may be difficult to do, you must take the time to look very, very closely at your product to identify the beauty and blemishes. There will be both.

3.3 Preliminary Product – Whattaya Got There?

At this point, you've learned all about the market (chapter 3) and based on what we've discussed in this chapter – developing your reason to be, designing your competitive advantages, understanding and protecting against your weaknesses – you should have enough background information to start fleshing out the design of your product and a strategy for presenting it to alpha test customers. Who?

→ Don't waste your time or money building what you think is a final version of the product at this point because it's likely to go through a number of changes before it's ready for the market.

→ Develop an inexpensive demo or as complete a drawing as you can. You also want to be sure to show and explain how the product is going to work.

→ Develop a written document that clearly quantifies the product's benefits.

→ Develop a preliminary pricing strategy so you'll be able to explain how much value your product provides.

The only reason to do all of this is so that you can begin receiving feedback from Alpha test customers, so let's find out who these folks are.

3.4 Alpha Test - Do They Like It, Do They Really Really Like It?

It's been a while now since you have had any contact with your market. You have been busy identifying prospect priorities, identifying your target market, and designing your preliminary product. It's now time to go back to the market to see what prospects think about what you've done and if you're still on track. At this point, you are not quite ready to start marketing and selling your product; it's still too early for that.

While many first time entrepreneurs get to this point and decide to begin marketing and selling their product, the vast majority will find out the hard way that their product is not ready for prime time. Unfortunately for them, they will have spent a lot of time and money to create a product that only minimally satisfies the market. In many cases, they lack the resources to go back and fix the problems.

But you're not going to make the same rookie mistakes they do. You know that there are still a number of important things you must do before your product is ready for the world and you're going to take a little more time to do it the right way. Determine depth and breadth of the problem or desire from the business or household. This means getting some feedback on how you're doing thus far.

It's never easy hearing negative comments (let's face it, nobody wants to be told they have an ugly baby), but this type of feedback is invaluable. And it is better to hear the negative now in the alpha test phase, before you've spent a lot of money building what you think is the final product only to find out after the fact that it has some major flaws. Consequently, you cannot be defensive when getting this feedback. If you are, prospects may not be willing to tell the truth; they'll just say what they think you want to hear.

How to Find Alphas?

So where do we find these alpha test customers? From your initial market survey, of course! As we recommended for the initial market research and will say again, make sure to keep track of the respondents who seemed the most interested. Not only are these people able to help you with you product, but they are future customers. Bring them along for the journey.

Who the alpha testers are largely depends on the kind of product you have.

→ If you are selling your product to a company, you want to do your best to make sure you meet with everyone who is impacted by the problem your product addresses, has a desire for what your product promises, or will use your product in any way.

→ If you are selling your product to a consumer, there might be multiple angles you'd want to test with multiple groups. For example, if you are selling a children's breakfast cereal, you should solicit feedback from children and their parents. While children will be most concerned about taste, parents might be looking for other features such as nutritional value. Both groups are important in the success of your product and thus in the alpha test.

You will generally want to line up at least three alpha testers. After you have identified the best prospective customers for your alpha test, contact them, explain what you're looking for, and tell them how they would benefit from being an alpha customer (for example, offer them a large discount on the product if they choose to buy it in the future).

"If you do this right, potential alpha testers will ask you if they can participate in your trials. Presented correctly, alphas will appreciate that they get the product customized to their specific circumstances."

Charlie

One more step: Before you meet with your alpha testers, develop a list of questions you need them to answer. Some of these questions will look familiar as they are questions you probably asked when initially looking at the market. The questions should focus on the following:

→ What are your alpha test customers' most important priorities?
→ How much does it cost them in lost time, money or effort today to not solve the problems/desires you're addressing?
→ Have they previously purchased a competitor's solution? If so, why? Are they happy with it? If not, why not? If they didn't buy a competitor's solution that was available, why not?
→ How easy do they think it is to use your solution? What would they change?
→ Do they have any recommendations?

At this point, you are prepared. Meet with the alphas, open your briefcase, lay out for them your preliminary product and begin the conversation. Make sure that you first identify any implications of problems and desires, and then and only then, bring up your proposed solution. Describe how the product works, its attributes, and how customers will benefit.

Ask your questions. The objective of your questions is to identify all possible quantitative and qualitative issues (so that you can address them later). Thank them very much for their time and offer to follow up with them because as we're sure you've already figured out, one of the primary goals of an alpha test is to sign-up beta test customers.

Step 4: Product Introduction

4.1 Pilot Product - Fixing the Problems

Armed with the information harvested from alpha testers, *now* you are ready to actually design your pilot product. While the alphas' feedback is irrevocably important, do not take everything that each and every one of your alpha test customers said as a mandate for change. You need to rank-order and prioritize their feedback as critical, nice to have, not important, something to consider for the next version, or not important.

Start by looking for patterns. If all of the alphas pointed out similar problems or offered the same recommendations, you should certainly consider the importance of each of them. If only a few highlighted certain issues or suggested improvements, you will have to determine if these issues relate specifically to this select group only, or whether the suggestions could be beneficial for all prospects. Remember, you're building your product to satisfy the majority of your target market, not everyone on the planet.

"Get your product out into the market as soon as possible. It doesn't have to be perfect. Just make sure it delivers sufficient value to your target market – and prove your concept." The longer you wait the more costly and difficult making changes to the product will be. Getting traction in the market is key."

Charlie

After reviewing all the suggestions and issues that came out of the alpha tests, do the following:

- → Make a list of issues identified with your preliminary product and put them in order from most severe to least.
- → Make a separate list of all recommendations made by the alpha test customers, ranking them from most valuable to least valuable.
- → Next to each issue and recommendation, explain what you'd have to do to make each of these changes (or improvements) in your product.
- → Next to each change/improvement estimate the amount of time and money you believe is required to make each of these changes.
- → Circle any change or enhancement that you are not comfortable that you have the skills to make. Put an estimate on how much each change will add to the cost of the product.

And when building your pilot product, you should include the following critical components:

- → ***Time is Money:*** How long is it going to take to either build your product or to get it from a vendor? The longer it takes to get your product to market the less likely your business will be successful. Because of delay, prospects may be able to find a solution from a competitor or a workaround.

→ **Skills:** Are you building a company that will have to actually develop/build the product in house? If not, where can you find these skills? How easy will it be to find the necessary skills? How much will it cost to get the skills (money, time, etc.)?

→ **Costs:** Do you have a complete picture of what your costs will be to build and offer your product or service?
- Variable Costs are costs you can control which gives you a better chance of increasing your gross margin. These include things like labor and materials.
- Fixed Costs are costs that, once incurred, are not subject to easy management. These include things like rent.
- Have you thought of ways to lower these costs?

→ **Pricing:** Have you developed your pricing strategy for your product/service? If so, how did you determine it?
- Cost plus
- Competitive analysis
- Value based
- Pulled out of thin air
- Estimating how long will it take your average customer to receive sufficient amount of benefits to justify the price

→ **Simplicity:** How easy is it for the average prospect to use your product/service?
- Complexity may mean that more individuals (at the prospect) will be involved in buying and/or implementing the solution.

→ **Budget:** Can you put together a budget that reflects all of these factors? Do you have the discipline to live by the budget?

4.2 Beta Test – Close Only Counts In Horseshoes and Hand Grenades

Now that you have built your pilot product, you are ready to go to market. The pilot product is really the market's first look at what you have. It is the first version released outside the organization. Whereas alpha tests examine theoretical concepts, beta tests are for products that are mostly complete. Beta testing involves a real trial of a real product. If you are selling software, a beta test would include installation of the software on the testers' computers for use over a period of time.

The purpose is to get people trying the actual product in hopes that they'll buy. Signing up beta test customers is a very big thing. This is your first customer. You can't afford to make mistakes because their success and satisfaction using your product truly determines your future. So let's make sure we do this right.

Michael

"When signing up beta test customers, have them sign an **engagement contract** that explicitly states what you are responsible for delivering. Otherwise, you could experience the dreadful consequences of **scope creep**. Scope creep results from beta testers asking for additional benefits and/or customization. These often cause unnecessary delay in getting to market and substantial cost overruns."

The goal of beta testing is very different from that of alpha testing. Your primary objectives are to make sure the pilot product works as promised, make it as easy to use as possible, and make sure that your customer is satisfied – or better yet, downright positively enthusiastic. If you identify any problems, fix them as soon as possible and deliver them to your beta customers.

What Else Do You Want From Your Beta Test?

Once Beta testers are happy, ask them for a letter of recommendations and a list of leads for you to call. As you can imagine, getting the right recommendation is an art. Even if customers really like your product, they don't frequently get around to writing recommendations. When they do, they may write weak or ineffective ones.

We suggest that you tell your customers that you know how busy they are and that, to make it easier for them, you've taken the liberty of writing a first draft for their review. Write the draft exactly as if they had done so. Present your draft and point out that they should feel free to make any changes they want. Most of the time, the customer will copy the letter verbatim onto their letterhead and return it to you, which is of course exactly what you wanted in the first place. If you have multiple beta testers willing to give you a recommendation, make sure each customer's response is unique and it highlights different benefits of your product.

Most new ventures rarely have the funds necessary to create a brand for the product. So, being clever, you leverage your customer's brands to boost the image of your product.

4.3 The Product – Another Piece Done

Take all that you've learned from the Beta tests, make any final changes to your product, and now you have a product that is ready for the market.

Conclusion

All products evolve as they are developed. Shaped and molded by what you learn from the market and your prospective customers, the best products take good ideas and turn them into great ones. Congratulations, your product is ready to go and now it's time to move on to the third and final component of building your successful business, the plan.

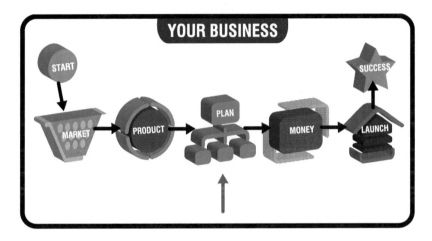

"The purpose of business is to create and keep a customer."

- Peter F. Drucker, Writer and Management Guru

"In business, one of the challenges is making sure that your product is the easiest to experience and complete a sale."

- Mark Cuban, Entrepreneur and Owner of the Dallas Mavericks

Objective

To show you how to plan, build, communicate, and manage a company to maximize profitability.

What You Need To Know About the Plan

Let's recap. So far, you have studied the market to determine what kind of needs and wants are out there, and you've begun to build and test a product that satisfies them. Now it's time to consider "the plan:" all the strategies and tactics meant not merely to support the sale of your product, but to significantly expand the reach, scope, and capability of your business. This may surprise you, but even with a great product that satisfies a high priority, without "the plan," the product will likely sit on the shelf somewhere and you'll have few customers. The plan is where entrepreneurs think and act "beyond the product". The plan extends from designing a company to tactical plans to realizing your goals through solid management and execution. As you see, success here has nothing to do with how great your product is nor how accepting is the market for it.

Here's an example of how your plan can greatly impact success in the most classic of entrepreneurial ventures: a lemonade stand (Fig. 5-1). Let's say that there are two lemonade stands in a given town and each is selling the identical product – freshly-squeezed lemonade made from 10 lemons, five tablespoons of sugar, and three cups of water. The two products taste exactly the same and are sold in the same exact white plastic cups. Yet one lemonade stand is raking in the cash while the other is losing money. How might you account for these differences?

Unique Business Model:
Instead of charging 25¢ per cup like most lemonade stands, they charge $1 for unlimited refills. Because it's so hot and the lemonade is so tasty, buyers love this.

Excellent Management:
Grandma was the former CEO of a famous soft drink company with 20+ years managing employees in the soft drink industry.

Superior Marketing Capabilities:
Katie, the young girl, has told her entire girl scout troop about the stand.

Ideal Location:
Sales have gone through the roof because the lemonade stand is right next to a big municipal park.

Better Operational Efficiency = Better Product:
Unlike the stand down the road which keeps the lemonade cold with ice cubes that quickly melt and dilute the taste, this stand has a mini-refrigerator in the stand which can hold up to 20 cups at a time for a truly cold, refreshing drink.

Lower Costs:
Thanks to Grandma's pre-retirement connections, she is able to purchase the lemons and sugar at a fraction of what they cost at the grocery store.

Here is another lemonade stand example that you might find more relevant. Umpqua, an Oregon-based bank, recently launched a marketing campaign called "Lemonaire," which is aimed at helping entrepreneurial kids start their first business: a lemonade stand. After filling out an application, children can pick up a free Umpqua Lemonade Starter Kit, which includes cups, napkins, a sticker, table cover, small business guide, and $10 in start-up capital. The point is to attract small business owners (perhaps the children's parents) to use Umpqua to finance their loans. A spokesperson for Umpqua explained, "We look for ways to hit people with a different mindset, and the lemonade stand is a perfect metaphor for what small business is about."[19] While they probably have the same rates for small business owners as the next bank, they used a unique strategy to attract customers. This made all the difference in their success.

---

[19] http://www.springwise.com/weekly/2007-07-18.htm#lemonaire

Like Umpqua using a clever marketing strategy to drive sales, this section is designed to show you all of the levers you can pull when building your plan.

What's The Story?
This chapter focuses on four major topics:

→ Determining where you want your company to go and how to best get there
→ Building a business model and tactics to support it
→ Communicating what you've built so that prospects know about it
→ Managing the execution of the process to ensure everything stays on track

We will help you to identify the right goals for your business, develop a distinctive business model, design high-impact marketing and sales tactics, employ sound management practices, and achieve operational efficiencies. Combined, these initiatives will help you maximize profitability and enhance the overall value of your business.

Why David Can Take On Goliath and Win
Many people mistakenly believe that in order to be successful, you have to be huge so that you can compete with the big guys. However, just like lemonade stands, most entrepreneurial ventures start out small. Steve Jobs and Steve Wozniak started Apple Computer in 1976 from the Jobs family garage when they were 20 years old. Ten years later, the company was worth $2 billion and had 4,000 employees.[20] But they started small. It can be intimidating to think about your competition and daunting to imagine how you're ever going to be able to contend with them, but rest assured, there are advantages to being the small player.

---

[20] http://news-service.stanford.edu/news/2005/june15/jobs-061505.html

Large companies, by their very nature, are not particularly entrepreneurial because they derive strengths from their assets (e.g. capital, brand/ image, extensive market presence, and the like) which give companies some significant advantages that entrepreneurs should not underestimate. Going head to head with them where they're strong and you're weak is ill advised. That said, it never ceases to amaze us how many new ventures think they can out-locate, out-market, or out-spend their larger competitors. It just doesn't work.

However, smaller companies can compete very effectively with their large counterparts by flanking them. A concept borrowed from the battlefield, a flanking strategy seeks to hit a competitor from the side (as opposed to head-on) in order to avoid direct confrontation. Typically, the move is swift and secretive, aiming to surprise the competition. And because you're not hitting their underbelly, hopefully they won't find your actions threatening enough to respond to. Here are three of the most common flanking strategies and why they work:

1. **Target Niches in Large Markets.** Find a small target market within a larger market that is currently being underserved by the major players. For example, if you thought that the market for travel guide books was saturated, think again. While there were books for families, frugal travelers, and the general population, Luxe City Guides were created for the ultimate upscale traveler by providing a "highly selective and opinionated lists of only the best shops, restaurants and hotels, [and] unique services and lifestyle options each city has to offer."[21] Niches frequently have slightly different priority needs and perceive value differently than the rest of their market. As such, they provide an excellent opportunity for a new venture or small business.

---

[21] http://luxecityguides.com/home.php?category_id=1

Why This Works

The bigger a company gets, the more difficult it is to consistently grow at the same rate that it did when starting out. A company with $1 billion revenues needs to generate $100 million in new sales in order to grow by 10%, whereas a company with $25 million in revenues only needs to grow by an additional $2.5 million to grow the same 10%. Simply put, small niches do not offer enough upside potential for large businesses. Where a small company can easily justify going after a $5 million market niche, a large business cannot because it would take at least 20 of these small markets (assuming they could get 100% of the sales) to reach $100 million new sales. It is very difficult for a larger company to manage 20 distinct customized products for 20 different markets at the same time, especially since their odds are much better by targeting one much-larger homogeneous market.

Which fish do you think your competition is most likely to go after? They're clearly unable to go after all of them so they will have to choose which can satisfy the greatest need at one time.

Fig. 5-2

Your Competition

You

2. **Getting to Market Sooner.** By their very nature, successful
   large companies have more to lose than smaller businesses.
   They understand far too well that a serious mistake could kill
   their golden goose and are consequently more risk-averse in
   their behavior. Their number one rule is to "do no damage."
   In minimizing their risk, large companies habitually
   over-analyze and make decisions very slowly. Managers tend
   to make decisions in groups, which gives the individuals
   cover, but also slows down the process even more. Important
   decisions usually require a minimum of six months to
   evaluate and an additional six to nine months to implement.
   This is an advantage for the smaller entrepreneurial venture.
   Instead of six months or more, the entrepreneur usually only
   needs a couple of hours or a few days to make an important
   decision. Actually, their whole decision process might be
   nothing more than asking a partner, "So Joe, what do you

think?" As a result, a small business could have entered a new market, sold their product, obtained references from customers, and received positive press from the industry journals before the large company even decides to get in the game.

Why This Works

The molasses-like decision making process at large companies is not the only place where small businesses have the upper hand. Here are some other areas in which the big guys are slow.

In talking with business leaders, we found that on average large businesses dedicate almost a third of their yearly staff time for planning and require between 6-12 months to begin implementing. In contrast, small businesses, on average, spend significantly less time on planning and usually only require 30-60 days to begin implementation. As a result, small businesses can come up with new strategies and tactics in about a third of the time it takes larger businesses to do the same. Additionally, we found that management at large companies can spend an inordinate amount of time in meetings, while in small businesses management spends just a small part of their day in meetings. This is time that can be used more efficiently to make things happen.

Charlie

"I have been at meetings at large companies where the sole purpose of the meeting was to determine where and when they were going to have the next meeting. Now that's productivity!"

3. **Changing Directions on a Dime.** Just as entrepreneurs can get to market quickly, they can also change directions quickly. If a product isn't working well or a variation on the product may work better, entrepreneurs can make a change well before a manager in a big company gets wind that there's even a problem.

Why This Works

Big businesses take years to get to where they are. Perhaps they started as one man entrepreneurial shops, but now their ranks are filled with middle managers who are more interested in keeping their jobs (and lavish salaries) than they are in taking chances. With every decision they make, there is a risk of losing what has taken years to build. One misstep can do irreversible damage to a company's brand and image in the marketplace. As such, everything has to be approved by everyone, a process commonly (and eloquently) known as "covering your ass." Large companies are famous for it and have a lot of asses to cover.

Planning: He Who Fails to Plan, Plans to Fail

Building the business strategy can be the most difficult task in starting a new venture. With previous experience in the planning process from corporate jobs, many entrepreneurs will roll their eyes at the mere mention of the words strategy, tactics, or planning. But the reality is that every successful business begins with a plan.

Those who have had experience with planning at large companies know all too well how it works in corporate America and remember how excruciating the process can be. Most Fortune 500 companies spend months planning – and most employees view it as a colossal waste of time. Companies spend inordinate amounts of time scrutinizing, analyzing, and reexamining every minute detail while burning the midnight oil night after night. After several weeks, the plan is finished, goes into a big binder, and begins its life on a dusty shelf never to be seen or used again.

In an entrepreneurial venture, the plan gets much more practical use.

You need a plan that describes how you intend to go from a two person operation in a garage to $20 million organization within three years. While we encourage you to think big, you also have to be realistic and also develop plans that are in sync with your personal goals and reality. For example, perhaps your long-term goal is to create a 10 person business that sustains and supports all of the employees, but to grow no bigger. Obviously, you can change your plan at any time as needed without having to receive approval from 14 layers of management, but simply thinking about how you are going to get from point A to point B and writing it down will help flesh out your path.

According to Harvard business professor Michael Porter, "There are no substitutes for strategic thinking. Improving quality is meaningless without knowing what kind of quality is relevant in competitive terms. Nurturing corporate culture is useless unless the culture is aligned with a company's approach to competing. Entrepreneurship unguided by strategic perspective is much more likely to fail than to succeed."[22]

Strategic planning requires that you transcend the day-to-day operations of the company and think big picture and longer-term. It's the process by which a company decides on its goals and how to best allocate its resources in order to accomplish those goals. Planning is important not only at the beginning of your business when you're deciding what kind of company you want, but it should be used

---

[22] Sicangco Cruz, Elfren. "The Rise of Strategic Planning." Business World 10 Jan 2006: S1/4.

regularly throughout the life of the business. Just some of the reasons to get a plan in order are:

→ *To get everyone marching to the same beat.* A plan offers employees a common focus, mutually agreed upon concrete goals, and a singular vision to rally around. Without established goals, new ventures tend to exhaust their limited resources by going in many different (and often scattered) directions. This leads to ineffective use of time and money.

→ *To identify shorter-term benchmarks and objectives.* Lofty long-term goals can be intimidating, while short-term objectives are much easier to digest. Establish short-term objectives to keep everyone moving in the same direction and to help build momentum for the journey.

→ *To divide the workload.* A plan enables a company to break down objectives into bite-size chunks that can then be assigned to different individuals. If you assign responsibility for a huge objective to more than one person, it likely won't get done. On the other hand, if you can divide the workload and assign individuals with different jobs that together lead to the end goal, they're more likely to accomplish their tasks. There is a tendency for individuals to expend less effort when working collectively than when working individually, according to a number of researchers who explored this concept and coined the phrase "social loafing."[23] For example, when a supermarket store manager told his eight floor clerks that they were all responsible for making sure that the shelves were neat and the floor was clean, no one took

---

[23] Charbonnier, Emmanuelle. "Social Loafing and Self-Beliefs." <u>Social Behavior and Personality</u> 1998:

responsibility. When he selected one person to clean aisles 1-4, another to clean aisles 5-8, and another to clean the backrooms, the floors were always clean and the shelves were always neat because each individual person was accountable for his or her own task. It's more difficult to assign accountability to a group.

→ *To determine the investment required and priority of each alternative.* A plan enables you to look at different strategic options in the context of the investments that they will require. Entrepreneurs can examine each option separately to ensure they're choosing the path that provides the biggest bang for the buck.

→ *To reflect.* Planning requires that you look inward at your company's internal strengths and weaknesses, and externally at opportunities and threats (often abbreviated as a SWOT analysis).

Good planning takes into account all of these factors and their potential impact on the success of your business.

Where the Planning Begins
Many people find the strategic planning process convoluted and confusing. But they can find their way by keeping in mind that good planning is not done in a vacuum; you should get as much input and advice from others as possible.

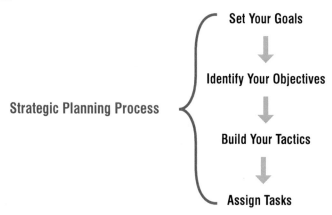

Strategic Planning Process

- Set Your Goals
- Identify Your Objectives
- Build Your Tactics
- Assign Tasks

Goals are the end-points and the long-term targets or aspirations for your business over 3-5 years. Goals must be both tangible and measurable, so that everyone in the company will be able to gauge progress based on these goals. We believe that a company's likelihood of reaching its goals is inversely related to the number of goals it identified. A company is most effective when it focuses on no more than three goals at any one time. The more goals a company focuses on, the more likely that these goals will at some point conflict with each other, making the entire ambitious package more difficult to accomplish. Examples of new business goals are: Becoming a major player in your market by selling to 250 clients (or 3% market share) by the end of the fourth year of business, generating $5 million in annuity revenues by the end of the fourth year, or realizing investor returns in excess of 25% per year by the end of the fifth year. Your goals can be more or less grandiose than these. The key is that they are realistically achievable in a three to five year timeframe.

Objectives are the specific, identifiable, and measurable points along the way that must be accomplished in order to realize the goal and can only be identified after management has agreed on the company's goals. There are no real requirements on the number of objectives you should have per goal – you may have as little as two or three objectives or as many as ten. Yet these provide management with a roadmap to track progress in achieving a company's goals. Since objectives are subsets of goals, they have shorter timeframes, ranging from as little as three months to as long as eighteen months. For example, if the company's goal was to sell 250 clients by the end of the fourth year, possible objectives could include: completing product development by the end of the 4th month, getting a successful beta test completed by the end of the 6th month, and signing the 40th client by the eighteenth month.

Tactics are the methodologies used to accomplish the venture's objectives. They don't represent points along the way like objectives, but they specifically describe how the company will achieve its objectives. Tactics are usually short-term, from less than one month to in some cases as long as 12 months. It is not unusual to see the same tactics repeated over and over again to achieve an objective. For example, if the objective of the company is to have 40 clients sold within eighteen months, possible tactics could include: Sending out 100 direct mail letters per month to qualified prospects starting in the 7th month, setting up 10 in-person sales calls per month by calling 100 prospects who received the mailing the month before, and closing an average of four sales per month as a result of presenting to 10 prospects per month.

Since new ventures and small businesses have significantly less money to spend on tactics than their larger competitors, they have do things smarter. Successful entrepreneurs use the following four litmus tests to prioritize which tactics to use. Tactics must be:

→ High impact
→ Cost-effective
→ Easy to implement
→ Easily monitored and measured

Tasks are the smallest components of the planning process. They are the day-to-day actions that taken together comprise the company's tactics. Similar to tactics, tasks are often repeated on a periodic basis. They are the easiest to manage because they have short time frames – requiring just hours up to one month. Since tactics may require months to accomplish, substantial time and money could easily be wasted on ineffective tactics. Tasks, on the other hand, are in effect early monitoring mechanisms. Since tasks are short in duration, a problem implementing them can be fixed quickly with little time or money wasted. For example, if a tactic is to mail out 100 direct mail pieces per month to qualified prospects, tasks could include: Designing the mailer marketing piece three weeks prior to the first mailing (by the first week in the sixth month), getting the letters and envelopes printed and letters inserted by the beginning of the last week in each month, and mailing the letters prior to the last three days of each month.

Building Your Business Model

A business model describes how a company does business and makes money. Some models are quite simple, such as a lemonade stand that charges $1.00 per cup of lemonade. Other models can be more complicated. Let's say, for example, that a lemonade stand didn't charge for the lemonade, but instead earned revenue through advertisements placed all over the stand: PTA ads, ads for Girl Scout cookies, ads for soccer league tryouts, and so on. The second stand would be earning money similar to the way that Google revolutionized the internet: advertisement-based revenue. Google developed a business model around query-based paid advertisements. The company sells "sponsored link" space to companies that tie advertisements to a user's specific search query. Typing "lemonade" into Google retrieves information, history, and stories about the sweet drink as well as paid links to sites where you could find recipe books for purchase.[24]

---

[24] Pappa, Michael. Managing the Digital Enterprise. Digitalenterprise.org/models/models_text.html

A good business model adds value to the product and enhances a company's profit potential. It can make a fair product good and a good product great. A bad business model can, quite simply, kill your company.

In addition to the business models identified above, here are some good examples of how other companies have used their business model to build competitive advantage:

The "Low Prices – All Under One Roof" Model

This model enables companies to provide lower perceived prices and greater convenience with one-stop shopping. This model enhances the product's attractiveness to consumers. Each of the following companies customized this basic model to maximize profitability:

→ *Costco* makes this model its own in two unique ways. First, most common products are sold in larger quantities, which lower the individual costs to consumers. Second, all customers have to purchase an annual membership in order to shop at Costco. These factors enhance Costco's image as a low cost retailer and make customers feel like they're part of a special, select group, while delivering above industry profit margins to the company.

→ *Supermarkets* maximize their sales and profits through a clever use of a loss leader business model. Pricing their milk, bread, and eggs (the most purchased products in the store) at or below cost, customers perceive that all the products at the store are similarly priced. Many customers come into the store to buy only the basic necessities, but end up also purchasing other highly attractive, high margin products, like paper goods, cleaning supplies, hair products, etc., which offsets any losses the store incurs on bread, milk or eggs.

The "Making it Easier to Buy" Model

The attractiveness of a product is not limited to the product itself. Companies that can make their product more accessible and available to customers usually sell their products at higher margins or sell additional services to go along with the product. Various businesses have customized this model, such as:

→ *Convenience Stores* use the flipside of the business model used by supermarkets. Selling the convenience of having everything just around the corner, available 24 hours a day, no lines, and the ability to get in and out quickly, these stores charge much higher prices than supermarkets for the convenience they deliver.

→ *Rooms To Go* promotes its ability to offer furniture to customers who don't have to pay for 12 months or longer. This is a highly effective tool for generating customer interest because everyone loves the fact that they get furniture now (immediate gratification) and don't have to pay until later. The company more than offsets the cost of this strategy through a combination of higher sales volume, lower product costs (due to higher volume), and inventory cost savings (due to fewer SKUs).

The "Low Entry Cost, High Margin Add-On" Model

Here, the business locks in new customers by selling the primary product or service below cost or at break-even, with the goal of selling complementary high margin products or services that are necessary to use the first product. This model is different from the supermarket model because the add-on products are the only ones that work with the first product.

→ *Hewlett Packard* sells printers at below their cost in order to sell their high margin ink cartridges that the printer requires. In most cases, supplemental ink purchases offset printer losses very quickly.

→ *Gillette and Schick* were famous for sending a free razor and disposable blade to most homes in America. They gave away the razor, but made their money on their razor blades since they were the only ones selling the blades that fit the razor. Gillette and Schick continue to use types of these promotions with each new razor introduction.

The "Give Away Access to Customers and Charge Businesses For Access To Customers" Model

This model has become very popular on the Internet. There are many successful entrepreneurial companies who have used this model very effectively, including Google, YouTube, Yahoo!, MapQuest, etc.

→ *Social networking sites* like Facebook, MySpace, and Friendster, which enable users to connect with other users based on location, school, or interests, have exploded over the past several years. These sites generate revenue through contextual and social search advertising. Because the sites have so much information about their millions of users (that the users themselves posted), the sites with great precision can identify individual needs and wants and connect users to companies that provide the answer through targeted advertisements.

Now that you have seen a number of different business model examples, you should begin thinking about one that would be the best for your business. Remember, it should be based on your company's strengths while making it easier for customers to buy the product and thus can help generate greater profits. Later in this chapter you will learn how to create your own business model.

Communicating: Spreading the Word

Let's revisit a concept that we introduced earlier – what makes a product attractive to consumers. If you'll recall from Chapter 3, there are three factors that contribute to a product's attractiveness.

Product Attractiveness = Priority x Value x Communication

Since we have already talked about priority and value in detail, we're going to focus on communication here.

Communication is the means by which you get the word out about your product and/or business. You may have a product that solves a high priority need and provides tremendous value, but if prospects don't know your product exists, it cannot be attractive to them and you business will be in trouble.

Marketing and sales are the main vehicles your business will use to communicate its message. These are the tools you will employ to get prospects to know that your product exists and then purchase it. Marketing and sales are part art, part science. There is art in the creativity of your message and the means by which it is communicated. The science, on the other hand, is in understanding how people (prospects) learn and knowing how to motivate them. The process is simple, but certain steps must be followed in order to maximize effectiveness. The process by which companies get prospects to buy are:

→ Grabbing attention
→ Generating awareness about your product
→ Creating interest in your product (focusing on priority)
→ Educating your prospects about the benefits of your product
→ Persuading prospects that your product offers sufficient value
→ Motivating them to purchase (making the risk of not purchasing, greater than the risk of purchasing)

Most successful entrepreneurs' credit marketing and sales as the reason for their success. Good marketing and sales can help level the playing field for many small businesses. Yet this effort doesn't have to come with a high price tag. Later in the chapter, we will show you how to use marketing effectively to enhance product attractiveness, increase your sales and thereby get the most out of your marketing dollars.

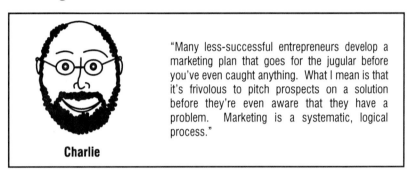

"Many less-successful entrepreneurs develop a marketing plan that goes for the jugular before you've even caught anything. What I mean is that it's frivolous to pitch prospects on a solution before they're even aware that they have a problem. Marketing is a systematic, logical process."

Charlie

The Map to the Plan

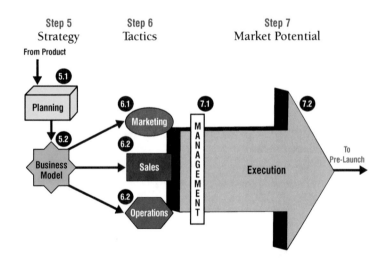

Step 5: Strategy

5.1 Planning – Keep Your Eye on the Prize

People often say they hate planning because this is where good ideas go to die. Planning has become synonymous with long nights of endless brainstorming, getting caught up in the minutiae of the process at the expense of the process itself, and just a painful ordeal that ends with esoteric babble and illegible scribbles that no one will ever see or use again. This is planning gone awry. You don't need umpteen days and complicated sessions to create a plan. We've actually come up with our own highly effective, heavily concentrated planning methodology. Instead of months, it can easily be completed in as little as only a day or two. To do this, we have divided the planning process into four separate sessions. The first two are primarily information gathering, while sessions three and four are specifically strategy driven.

"To all of you perfectionists out there: Don't be dead-set on trying to get the best plan when you have a good enough plan and can move along."

Michael

Session 1:
Identifying Company's Goals
(Estimated Time Requirement: 2 – 4 Hours)

Identify those individuals who should attend the session making sure to include multiple perspectives – both employees with different job functions and at various levels within the company. While we recommend having an experienced facilitator run the session, the senior manager can do it if costs are a concern. Also, the meeting should preferably be recorded; if video or audio equipment is not available, at least one person should be the designated note-taker.

Each participant should be instructed to do "pre-thinking" and come to the table with his or her own list of what they believe the company's top three goals should be. Ideally, this should be both obtainable and worthy of pursuing. They can range from "pie in the sky" ideas such as becoming the best diet chocolate chip muffin company in the Southeast U.S to benign year-end revenue goals for the next five years. Participants should be prepared to justify why these goals are most important and also to specify the obstacles in reaching them.

Begin the first session by writing every person's goals and issues on a separate page of easel-sized paper than can be taped to the wall of the room. The page might look something like this (Fig. 5-4):

Fig. 5-4

Planning Group Goals/Issues

Participant's Name: _____

Goals:			Issues:		
Yr. 1	**Yr. 3**	**Yr. 5**	**Yr. 1**	**Yr. 3**	**Yr. 5**
1)	1)	1)	1)	1)	1)
2)	2)	2)	2)	2)	2)
3)	3	3)	3)	3)	3)

After everyone has presented their list of goals, open the floor to questions and comments. T he objective of this session is to bring up issues that have not yet been mentioned.

"Caution! The most senior people in the room should be instructed to wait until everyone else has had a chance to ask their questions and make their comments. This will ensure that participants are not unduly influenced by the more senior participants – this is crucial for a successful meeting."

Michael

All questions should be invited, but overly-negative statements and comments should be avoided. Once everyone has had a chance to ask their questions and make comments, the facilitator should then instructs each person to write down what they now believe should be the company's top goals for first, third and fifth year-end.

"These types of meetings rarely end in unanimous agreement. In fact, we're happy when there are no fist fights. All that is required is that everyone agrees that these will be the company's goals and everyone will do their best in helping the company accomplish them."

Charlie

The facilitator collects these lists and takes another piece, which is split into three columns for years 1, 3, and 5. One by one, the facilitator will announce each goal identified by the participants (without revealing who came up with what). When a goal is mentioned more than once in the same year, the leader should put the corresponding number of times it has been mentioned in front of the goal. This process is repeated for the other years.

It is important to build consensus at this point. The facilitator should ask if anyone does not agree with these goals or believes that they cannot commit to their realization. Otherwise, the group will be considered in agreement on these goals and ready to move forward.

Session 2:
Identifying The Company's Strengths and Weaknesses
(Estimated Time Requirement: Approximately 1-2 Hours)

The entrepreneurial roadside is littered with unsuccessful entrepreneurs who really should have succeeded. Many lost track of their strengths (or never knew they had any) and could subsequently never fully exploit them to build competitive advantages. Just as importantly, companies need to know their weaknesses.

Strengths come in many different forms, such as the firm's structure, resource availability, or what special and unique capabilities it has developed. For example, a company's most important resource could be through its management's contacts with major players in the market. Using these connections, the company is able to get a head start and solicit market-leading references and obtain positive public relations spots.

Weaknesses – those things that the company does not do well – also come in many different forms. They can likewise be related to the firm's structure, resource availability, and capabilities. For example, a software company that doesn't have the technical expertise to program a certain kind of code for a new product will be at a disadvantage relative to a close competitor who does have this capability. Poorly designed software code leads to more complaints from customers, and consequently higher costs. This spiral effect then leads to higher prices and fewer sales or lower profits. If only you had recognized that your company did not have the necessary expertise, you could have hired an expert and spent a little more now to save a whole lot later.

With this in mind, ask participants to describe what they believe to be the company's strength and weakness in each of the following areas (Fig. 5-5):

Fig. 5-5

	Strengths	Weaknesses
Product:		
Marketing:		
Sales:		
Management:		
Pricing:		

With this information, the group can:

1. Develop a comprehensive list of the company's strengths and weaknesses
2. Identify the top two or three most important strengths that can help the company succeed
3. Brainstorm how each of these strengths can be put to use for the company's advantage and in as many places as possible throughout the business
4. Identify all weaknesses that can have a materially negative impact on the company's future

Session 3:
Developing the Company Vision
(Estimated Time Requirements: 2-3 Hours)

A company's vision statement telegraphs why prospects should buy, customers should buy more, employees should work hard, investors should invest, and lenders should lend. A lofty ambition, yes, but this is your company's rallying cry. A company's vision statement is often confused with the more familiar mission statement, but a mission statement describes the company's values and principles. A vision statement puts in plain words how the company conducts business to make money.

It is much more than a bunch of words; it's a tool to keep everyone in the company in sync, set priorities, and maintain focus. A company's vision will no doubt change over time as the company evolves, but it's most important to establish a vision when a company is just starting out. This should relate back to the product's reason for being that you developed in Chapter 3.

In developing your company's vision there are a couple of best practices we recommend:

→ The vision statement should be no more than 20 words
→ The vision statement should be clear of "buzz words" or clichés

Begin by everyone in each aspect of your business separately completing the following form (Fig. 5-6).

Fig. 5-6

> **In the spaces below, please explain how our company can uniquely deliver more value to each of the following constituencies than our competitors can. Keep in mind cost and reasonableness:**
>
> **Prospects:**
>
> **Customers:**
>
> **Employees:**
>
> **Investors:**
>
> **Lenders:**
>
> **Vendors:**
>
> **Other (If it relates specifically to your business):**

Break the participants into smaller groups for brainstorming. Each group should synthesize its individual statements into one group statement for each of the company's constituencies. Each group should then present to all. Based on new insights that may have come from hearing from everyone, participants should go back into groups and develop one vision statement for the company. This could be a challenging process and often times, coming up with one statement that speaks to all of the constituencies in impossible. If that's really the case, the most important constituencies are prospects and employees, so base your statement around them. It is best to get as many people involved in this process as possible. Anyone who can offer insight, has a unique perspective, vested interest or has market knowledge would be a plus.

"No, we're not kidding about the 15 words or less. It's crucial. With 15 or fewer words your statements will have the substance it needs to get your point across, but it will also be simple to remember and capable of standing out. It will also force you to refine your grandiose visions to a core idea."

Charlie

Session 4:
Agreeing On Objectives
(Estimated Time Requirement: 1-4 Hours)

The final step in this highly concentrated planning process is developing the company's objectives. Remember, these are time-specific, but do not describe a process or an action (that's what tactics are). Based on each stated goal, brainstorm what objectives can best move the company toward the target. After the group has agreed on what objectives to pursue, the group should determine a realistic timeline for each. While there is no limit to the number of objectives per goal, we have found that as the number of objectives gets larger (usually over 10) these start to look more like tactics.

5.2 Business Model – The Key to a Model Business is a Good Business Model

Remember, the business model is how the company does business to generate revenue – how it prices its product, sells it, services it, etc. An effective business model can simultaneously increase the benefits and reduce the risks of your product to enhance the overall value to prospects.

"A good business model makes your product as easy to buy as possible."

Charlie

As background for building you business model, follow these initial steps:

1. Think about what you can do to leverage your competitive advantages into your product's offering. Notice that we used the word "offering" here. Offering includes the product and everything else associated with getting prospects to buy.

2. List every negative quantitative and qualitative factor associated with your product. Take some time and consider what you can do to minimize the negative impact of these on your prospects. As you do this, keep in mind that reducing negatives (costs) increases total value.

To help explain how to develop a unique business model, we are going to use a fictional company as an example.

The company, Superior Medical Solutions, Inc. (SMS), has developed a revolutionary way to process, disinfect and dispose medical waste such as needles, blades, scalpels and other sharps. The product, called the Zapper, is a small machine that fits into a surgical suite, hospital room or physician's examination room. Using a patented process, the Zapper exposes the discarded sharp to incredibly high temperatures to reduce the volume by 98% and then ultraviolet light to kill the germs.

Costs/Benefits:

→ The device reduces accidental needle sticks by over 60%, which will save the average hospital on average over $80,000 on treatment costs and disposal alone per year. Sharps are currently disposed of in biohazard trash receptacles.

→ The cost to put the system throughout the average size hospital is $120,000.

→ The device lasts about six years before it has to be serviced, which will cost the hospital $15,000 at the time of service.

While a hospital can earn a return on their investment of more than 400% over six years, few hospitals are interested in buying the product. The primary reasons were:

→ *Cost:* The vast majority of hospital CFOs did not have the $120,000 in their budget for this.

→ *Credibility:* SMS is unknown and prospects are unsure the company will be around to service the product in the months and years to come.

→ *Concern:* Hospitals were not convinced that the product could really destroy all the germs to a safe level.

To address these issues, the company looked at their competitive advantages, which included being well capitalized and having a prestigious board member with a national reputation with hospitals. Leveraging these advantages and others, the business developed the following **_new_** business model – which responds to the main reasons hospitals weren't buying.

→ **_Reducing Cost:_** The Company will lease the product to the average hospital for $30,000 per year for a minimum of 5 years, which includes all servicing. Leasing the product satisfies the cost issue because the product delivers over 200% return to the hospital within the same budget year.

→ **_Enhancing Credibility:_** The Company looked into having established medical device companies distribute the Zapper under their own private labels. Selling the Zapper to these intermediaries and then having these companies sell it into hospitals helped SMS overcome its lack of credibility in the marketplace. SMS believed that hospitals would likely pay the higher cost associated with buying through a middleman and accept a lower (but still very attractive) return on their investment in order to "buy credibility". While this approach would yield less money per unit sold, the incremental volume sold would more than compensate for this.

→ **_Offsetting Concern:_** The Company hired a very famous and well-established medical school to confirm the product's effectiveness and longevity. SMS used the school's name and testimonials throughout their sales and marketing literature. While the company had little to no credibility in the market, it began building goodwill through leveraging a third party's strong brand.

Step 6: Tactics

6.1 Marketing – Spreading the Word

Marketing is the basic tool that gets your salespeople in the door or your customers in the store. With the explosion of Internet, cable TV, and alternative media over the past ten years, the average cost of getting face-to-face with prospects has increased considerably. With the sheer number of companies vying for attention and advertisers using any and every opportunity to grab attention, consumers are quite overwhelmed. Consequently, while effective marketing is more important now than ever before, it is also more expensive and difficult to execute.

Marketing in entrepreneurial ventures is very different from that in large companies. Fortune 500 companies primarily use marketing as a way to leverage their strong brand to successfully introduce new products and product extensions. Entrepreneurial ventures, however, do not yet have any brand equity and typically launch just one product. For these ventures, getting the biggest bang for the communication buck comes by:

→ Building a unique marketing message
→ Creating a good product/company related story that resonates with prospects
→ Positioning the company as the value leader

The Message is what you want targeted prospects to hear, understand, and ultimately act on. While this sounds simple, the reality is that most companies' messages are "lost in translation" because they are overly complex, abstract, obvious, gimmicky, or boring.

In building a message, use the vision statement that you developed through the planning process. If you have done a good job describing – succinctly – who you are and your reason for being, you already have the meat for your marketing message.

For a message to be effective, it must be clear, simple, memorable, and relevant. That's all there is to it. However, we see first-time entrepreneurs making the same mistakes with their message time after time.

→ First, the entrepreneur develops a message that fails to resonate with the intended audience because he created a marketing message from *his own perspective*. The problem is that the target market often has a different perspective.

→ Second, the entrepreneur develops a message that does not stand out from the rest. Let's face it, a message that presents one more virtually identical reason to do something is not one that will get people out of their seats and talking about you. Trying to be like everybody else will accomplish nothing. Be different, better, unique or be gone.

The Story is one of the most underrated, yet most effective, tools in your marketing toolbox. A story can transform an otherwise undifferentiated message into something that stands out entirely because the power of the story comes from its ability to generate emotions.

Storytelling is "the ability to place facts in context and deliver them with emotional impact," says Daniel Pink in A Whole New Mind. Pink suggests that in today's world, facts, hard logic, and bullet points are ubiquitous. From the PowerPoint presentations to the ability of anyone and everyone to find the GNP of Ghana with a few keystrokes on the computer, facts don't sell anymore.[25]

---

[25] Pink, Daniel. A Whole New Mind. Riverhead Books: New York: 2005.

Cognitive scientist Mark Turner writes, "Narrative imagining – story – is the fundamental instrument of thought. Rational capacities depend on it. It is our chief means of looking into the future, of predicting, of planning, and of explaining... Most of our experience, our knowledge and our thinking is organized as stories."[26] Humans are hardwired to remember stories; not facts.

The best stories touch people's emotions in a powerful way and become memorable. Just think about your favorite movies or books – the ones that left a lasting imprint on you. Those were probably the ones with stories that most directly spoke to you. Stories that are personal and believable soar. Those about overcoming fear, challenging a bully, or proving something everyone told you couldn't be done make people feel good. This gives your prospects something more relatable. In a commercial sense, it's not about the product anymore; it's the story around the product that becomes significant. Because stories can have personal impact, they often generate word-of-mouth buzz – the chats between family, friends, and colleagues that spread messages like viruses. Word-of-mouth buzz is Nirvana in the marketing world. It's free, it comes from a trusted source, it generates action, and once again, it's free.

Here an example of a very effective story:

In 1967, Maytag Corporation, maker of household appliances including washers and dryers, introduced the public to the Maytag Repairman as part of its marketing strategy. The premise of this character was to reinforce the notion that Maytag appliances were so reliable that the repair man had nothing to do. The public really connected with this character because he looked like "everyman", not some leading actor in Hollywood. He wore a blue collar uniform, was bored with his job, and just wanted to have customers who needed him. Bottom line:

---

[26] Turner, Mark. The Literary Mind: The Origins of Thought and Language. Oxford University Press, 1996.

We remembered him and Maytag appliances. Were Maytag appliances that much more reliable than the competition? We couldn't find any evidence that they were. But Maytag had sold us a great, great story.

While there are a number of ways to tell a story, public relations (PR) delivers more marketing credibility and bang for the buck than any other marketing venue. Consumers are jaded by advertising and no longer trust assertions made by ads on TV or in print like they did in the 1950s and 1960's. Today, they are much more likely to be swayed by articles written about products in credible sources or certified reviews like those found in Consumer Reports. Public relations is a great medium because it attempts to sway public opinion outside of what you would typically consider an advertisement. Often times, you will read a newspaper article and won't even realize that it was the offspring of a company's PR effort.

Generating positive PR for your company is easier to do than most new entrepreneurs realize. There are a number of techniques such as press conferences and free product demos for journalists, but we have found that a highly targeted approach works best. Hiring a PR firm with specific industry experience and contacts with specific journalists can get you a long way for a little money. Otherwise, you can go at it alone by identifying which industry journals are read by most of your prospects and attempt to write an article about your product for that journal. Certainly an overt sales pitch in a 500 word article is not going to make the cut, but you can easily write something that craftily masks your intention to sell something and instead offers advice, insight, a look at trends, etc. You have to find some kind of angle that introduces your product in a creative way that readers (not to mention the journal's editorial board) will find interesting and novel.

Contrary to popular belief, industry journals do not typically have a staff of journalists. Their staff is primarily in the business of getting advertising, so they rely heavily on outside writers contributing content to the journal.

When the article is published, your job is not quite done. Don't rely on your prospects to notice it; the article is a great way to build not just brand recognition, but also credibility.

Positioning is how you want prospects to perceive your company relative to competitors. Once again, highlighting a small difference between you and the other company is not going to be enough to get anybody excited. But don't get confused by this statement. We're not saying that your product has to be drastically different from your competitors. We're suggesting that there must be a big difference in the way your product is perceived compared to your competitors' products.

Charlie

"If you're going to use advertising, one of the most effective ways to do so is to position your company against the competitors in your market with the best reputations. The objective here is not to go head to head with them, but to use their well known reputation as a baseline to highlight your advantages. Hyundai does this exceptionally well by highlighting where they're better than Lexus, Mercedes and BMW, at a fraction of the price. Hyundai benefits by these comparative associations even though they're targeting an entirely different market segment."

A patent-pending label is another example of how a company can position itself. Many companies, large and small, apply for a patent on their product knowing full well that they probably will not get it. You may think that they are wasting their time and money on the application, but they're actually creating an image about their product and company. A stamp of patent-pending implies new and improved; it signals a better product. The company gets all this for around $10,000. Not bad.

Before you build your marketing tactics (your advertising strategy, public relations strategy, positioning strategy, lead generating, etc.) we recommend that you explore the following resources:

→ The Tipping Point by Malcolm Gladwell. Little, Brown and Company: New York. 2000
→ Crossing the Chasm by Geoffrey A. Moore. HarperCollins, New York. 1991

Pricing impacts much more than just profit margin; it influences perceptions. Set your prices low and the market will think that you're cheap. Increase your asking price, but offer the product on sale, and all of a sudden, prospects think that they're getting a good deal. Pricing is tricky.

Entrepreneurs who have done their homework often assume that prospects have also done their homework. These entrepreneurs have been analyzing competitors' pricing strategy and know precisely how much each company in the industry charges for a given product. In reality, however, while prospects probably have a ballpark idea of how much they pay for products, they often don't know the exact price. What's more is that prospects really have no idea what the price should be. You would think that companies would take advantage of this lack of knowledge and charge a premium, but actually, most new companies under-price their products and rarely benefit from it.

Charging low or high prices?

If prospects perceive a low-priced product category, they're more likely to buy one of the higher priced options within the category. They "trade-up" because the incremental cost of doing so is not material. They do this because, in their own way, it makes them feel better about themselves.

On the other hand, if a product category is perceived to be expensive, pricing becomes more complicated. Higher prices must be reinforced with greater perceived benefits, but be careful: Charging a high price in order to "buy" a quality image is short-sighted if your product can not deliver on those benefits.

What about the free lunch? New entrepreneurs often ask about giving away their product to get initial customers. There's no simple answer, but we normally caution against doing this. When customers get things for free without any agreed upon requirements from them, they tend to devalue them. Bottom line: These customers are poor references and usually major time-wasters.

Given your particular market, you may believe that pricing your product low is the only way to stimulate sales. However, an interesting alternative is allowing a third party with perhaps more credibility in the market sell your product for you, even under their name. This enables you to charge a higher price and increase total sales, which will more than pay for your partner's share. We talked about value added resellers (VARs) in Chapter 5 and this is a situation in which that relationship may make very good sense.

The pricing alternatives we've talked about thus far related to raising or lowering prices. Many entrepreneurs assume that these are the only pricing alternatives, but there are others. Instead of trying to make your product more attractive by lowering price, you might consider: Offering a payment schedule that better mirrors your prospects' budget constraints, leasing your product, tying your price to performance, offering a trial period, or any number of other creative pricing strategies. Remember, your success is tied to making it as easy as possible for your prospects to buy your product. If you do this correctly, your product's pricing will be perceived by your prospects as a benefit instead of a cost. And that's a homerun.

6.2 Sales – Reeling Them In

There is nothing more satisfying than making that sale. Sales are the Holy Grail to businesses. Without them, the company will fail. It stands to reason that the easier it is for a company to sell its products, the more successful it likely will be.

Internal sales tactics are capabilities that a company builds from within.

These include: how attractive the product is (based on Product Attractiveness = Priority x Value x Communication), the effectiveness of its sales force, and how easy the product is to buy.

→ **Product Attractiveness:** We've chiseled away on this concept throughout the book, especially in analyzing how you look at your market while building your product. This is the first hoop through which your product must jump in order to have any chance of being sellable. Does it respond to a high priority need or want? Does it provide value? Does anyone know about it?

→ **Sales Force Effectiveness:** In part, the communication part of product attractiveness largely depends on the quality and effectiveness of the company's salespeople. New ventures have a greater likelihood of succeeding when hiring talent with proven track records and connections within their market. While your company will have to pay a premium for these people, the benefit of growing sales quickly will more than compensate for the additional cost. This is not a place where being cheap pays off. Since nothing gets customers to buy faster than other customers buying, bringing successful sales people on board early can pay huge dividends in generating future incremental sales. By the way, the really good sales people you're looking for are not normally the ones unemployed and answering your classified ads. You've got to find out who the players are and then "borrow", ok, steal them. Make sure they are not bound by a non-competition agreement. A common mistake first time entrepreneurs make is hiring mostly low-cost, unproven sales people when they do not have the time or expertise to train them or wait for them to get productive. The best salespeople give prospects a sense of urgency to act. It is human nature to put off decisions as long as possible, but urgency can turn low- interest prospects into high-interest early adopters. The key is that there must be a high cost for prospects not to act. Salespeople create urgency through limited time offers or market exclusivity agreements and insinuate that if a prospect does not buy now, perhaps their competitor down the street will. The implied threat that a competitor will have the upper-hand because of this purchase could be all that is required to generate urgency.

→ *Location:* The old adage is still as true today as it ever was. One of the most important factors for success in a business is location, location, location. In retail, the way to make it easiest for people to buy is to be where they are. If you are in a retail business, don't be foolish and try to save a little money by getting a cheaper location (new entrepreneurs do it all the time, and it's one of the primary reasons for a retail stores to go under). There is a reason that rent on one retail location is more expensive than another; more people see it everyday. The more prospects that pass it, the more opportunities there are for sales. A good location is the best marketing and sales tool you can have in retail

External sales tactics are those capabilities that a company can build from the outside. The external sales tactics that can have a material impact on company sales include value added resellers (VARs) and strategic partners.

→ ***Value Added Resellers (VARs):*** VARs are companies or individuals who make a living selling other companies' products to their target market. This is very common in industries such as healthcare and finance. If we go back to our example of Superior Medical Solutions (SMS) and the Zapper, a VAR would be a company that sells medical equipment or medical supplies to hospitals. A company who sells syringes and needles is thereby also selling a product which can dispose of those sharps. For SMS, the benefit is the ability to get in front of the hospital purchasing department. There are both positives and negatives associated with a VAR strategy. On the plus side, VARs offer the ability to establish a large sales presence in many different geographic markets overnight with relatively low input costs. However, the downside is that VARs charge exorbitant commission rates and your product is just one of a slew of products the salespeople are promoting. By outsourcing sales to VARs, your product is not likely to get the attention in the market that you require, but you're effectively giving up control of the sales process. That said, VARs can be a good option for some new ventures with very high-margin products that do not require a long sales cycle or very sophisticated expertise of their salespeople.

→ ***Strategic Partners:*** Strategic partnership for via contractual agreements, usually between a large business (which has a sizable sales team) and a small business (which owns the rights to a unique product). An effective strategic partnership can elevate a small business to the big leagues overnight; a poorly chosen or ineffective partnership, however, can destroy value for both companies. Of the thousands of strategic partnerships formed each year, only a small percentage of them really work. The main reason why they falter is that they don't deliver enough value to the larger company and the salesperson at the larger company selling the product. If, on the other hand, the larger company can sell more of its own product as a result of selling the smaller company's product, the strategic partnership will be a win for both.

In addition to the factors above, there are two more sales related tips we believe can be very important in your company's success:

→ **Low Hanging Fruit:** Some might argue that there's not much sport in selling to the most interested prospects first. We couldn't disagree more. We're always amazed how this doesn't occur to many first time entrepreneurs. There are always going to be prospects that are more likely than others to be interested in your product. Prioritize them and sell to them first. They may not all be marquee-name customers, but they bring credibility. And, oh yes, cash.

→ **Purchase Chain:** The purchase chain is the combination of every buying entity that has to agree to purchase the product before it's even available for sale to the end user. For example, it's one thing to assume that customers will buy your product at supermarkets, but quite another actually to get supermarkets to sell your product. An entrepreneur that doesn't fully understand the implications of their product's purchase chain is at considerable risk. For many products, assuming your end user is your only customer is foolhardy. Take a moment and look at every entity in your purchase chain that could impact your sales.

Budgeting

After reading about marketing and sales, you may have wide eyes and wider aspirations of how you intend to communicate with the market about your product. Budgeting will help you determine how much you can actually spend on this process. To help you determine you budget for marketing and sales, we've developed the following tools:

→ Communication Budget Allocation Model
→ Revenue Maximization Tactics

Communication Budget Allocation Model

The companies that are most successful at attracting new customers are those that understand how to maximize the effectiveness of their limited marketing and sales budgets. For a company to do this, they first must determine how much money they have to spend per new customer on marketing and sales.

The first step is determining what your total average revenues per customer will likely be over a given period of time (e.g. usually a contract term). For example, assume that you're selling alarms and monitoring services to households.

First: Basic Information

→ You project that your average customer will pay $3,500 for the monitoring equipment you will be installing, including the installation cost.

→ Customers will pay $35.00 per month for your 24/7 system monitoring services.

→ Customers must sign a 30 month contract for the services.

So, Total Revenue (value) per new customer is projected to be $4,550 [$3,500 + ($35 x 30 months)].

Second: Gross Margin

→ Subtract out direct costs associated with the customer. These are costs that can be identified and directly assigned to the activities relating to one specific customer. In this case they are:

- Equipment costs: $850
- Initial cost of installation: $870 ($750 for salaries and $120 for truck and gas)
- Direct cost of monitoring the system/month: $9.75/month or $292.50 total

So, total direct costs per customer are $2,012.50 ($850.00 + $120.00 + $292.50).

This will leave your company with a gross margin, the difference between revenue brought in from the customer and the direct costs to service him, which in this case is $2,537.50 ($4,550.00 - $2,012.50).

Third: Net Margin

→ From the gross margin, subtract out all indirect costs associated with this customer. These are other costs that the company incurs which can't be traced directly to one customer. In this case, for example, indirect costs are rent, salary and benefits for technicians and receptionists, insurance, utilities, management, etc. The company has to account for and cover these costs somehow, so they allocate a portion of these direct costs to their customers.

→ Let's assume that the company's total indirect cost per month is $15,650.

→ The company projects an average of 600 companies per month using their service during the period of the contract, or an average indirect cost per month of $26.08 per customer ($15,650/600 = $26.08).

→ Total indirect costs per customer are $782.40 ($26.08 x 30 months) per customer over the length of the contract.

We will call the result of subtracting the indirect cost from the gross margin the net margin for the purposes of this exercise. ($2,537.50 - $782.40 = $1,755.10).

Fourth: Profit Margin

→ From the net margin, subtract out your desired profit margin as a percentage of revenue. This is somewhat arbitrary – and you can easily find the typical profit margins for similar companies in your industry, but for this example let's assume a 20% profit margin.

→ If each customer contributes $4,550 in revenue/month, 20% of that is pure profit for the company.

So, the profit per customer each month is $910 (20% x $4,550).

Fifth: Budget

→ Finally, subtract your desired profit margin from your company's net margin to determine how much money is available in total marketing and selling costs to acquire a new customer. In this case it is $845.10 ($1,755.10 - $910.00).

Revenue Maximization Tactics

Given the above example, your company would have $845.10 to allocate for sales and marketing per new customer, or a total of $507,060 ($845.10 x 600) to sell to the 600 customers projected above in the first year. This translates into an average of $16,902 ($507,060/30) per month.

Now you have to determine how to best use this $16,902 to acquire an average of 20 (600/30) new customers per month. This $16,902 has to be divided between marketing, advertising, and sales. The best way to do this is to work backwards.

1. Estimate how many qualified leads it should take to sell one new customer. Just to be conservative, we estimate 10 qualified leads. Assuming we need to add 20 new customers a month, and we need 10 qualified prospects for each new customer, we will need to generate 200 (20 x 10) qualified leads per month. Conservatively assuming that we need five leads for every qualified lead, we would need a total of 1,000 new leads per month to generate 20 new sales. The best way to get accurate numbers for these estimations is joining the relevant industry association and requesting access to their research.

2. Determine how much each marketing/sales option we have in our bag of tricks would cost us to generate (these numbers would normally come from a comparative test you might have run or from experience):
   → Web-based Cost/Lead: $4.25
   → Magazine Ads Cost/Lead: $6.11
   → Telemarketing Cost/Lead: $5.22
   → Direct Mail Cost/Lead: $3.95
   → Plus an allocated brochure cost of $1,000 per month

Assume for this example that you can use direct mail to generate leads, and thus your average cost per lead is $3.95. As such, you would have to spend $3,950 per month in order to generate the 1,000 nonqualified leads per month you need. Assuming you have to spend an additional $5.00 per qualified lead to convert non-qualified leads to qualified leads this would cost an additional $1,000 per month ($5.00 x 200 qualified leads) + ($1,000 per month for brochures) for a total marketing/advertising cost of $5,950 ($3,950 + $1,000 + $1,000 = $5,950) per month.

This would leave your company with $10,952.00 ($16,902 - $5,950) a month to cover all direct sales cost or $547.60 per new customer sold. Is this sufficient to pay the sales force salaries, commissions, and to cover direct and indirect sales expenses? If you have two sales people with a base of $36,000 fully loaded you would have already spent a total of $6,000 before commissions leaving you $3,352.00 for commissions per month or approximately $167 ($3,352/20) commission per sale. If this is not sufficient you either have to determine a way to acquire more than 20 new customers per month with the same amount of cost, raise your price per customer, lower your operating costs, or accept a smaller profit margin per sale.

6.3 Operations – Oil the Engine

There is a renewed focus on operations management in the business world. Not since the Ford Motor Company pioneered the assembly line in the early 1900's have there been such dramatic changes in operations management. With firms outsourcing virtually everything from production to call centers, companies big and small are discovering new ways to streamline processes and increase efficiency.

A new venture should outsource when something can be done cheaper, faster, or if the process requires significant overhead investment to do it in-house. While most of the buzz about outsourcing revolves around production plants in China and Mexico or call centers in India, there is also domestic outsourcing, in which companies essentially "buy help" in areas where they don't have core competencies. A company should not outsource if your company can do it better or if the process is central to your competitive advantage. If you can outsource a process for the same price and quality as you can produce in-house, this most likely is not a competitive advantage.

Operations management, however, is a much bigger area than just answering the outsourcing question. Focusing on what are often considered "back office" functions, "ops" is all about managing the systems that produce and distribute products. Sure, identifying suppliers, controlling inventory, ensuring consistent production quality, and designing distribution channels might not be the sexiest part of the business; we assure you that there is tremendous value to be gained or lost through management of operations.

Step 7: Implementation

7.1 Management – Who's the Boss?
Talk to any venture capitalist or seasoned investor and sure enough, they will always ask the same first question about your business: the management. They know that good management is fundamental to building successful businesses. In fact, given the choice, they are much more likely to invest in a company with strong management and less than great (but improvable) product, than one with mediocre management and a great product. They really want both, but the quality of management takes precedence in their decision-making process.

Everyone harps on the need for effective management today, but beyond the buzzwords, what is it? The reason top managers are paid the big bucks is because they have a track record of not just accomplishments but of doing so on time and within budget. They handle tough situations and crises calmly and methodically. They lead and motivate others. They have a unique ability to listen – to employees, customers, and investors. They make tough decisions and know a little about everything, but are wise enough to ask for help.

In an entrepreneurial venture, there are five keys to successful management:

1. **Building the Team:** Management is responsible for hiring the right employees for the job and bringing them together as a team. Hiring the right people is only half the battle; someone must bring everyone together and lead the troops. Leaders share several qualities – passion for the business, acting as chief cheerleader for employees, and inspiring focus, loyalty, and exceptional work. Every now and again, you're going to hire someone who turns out to be a poor fit for your company. One disgruntled or ineffective employee can destroy all you've built by damaging and possible commitment of others. Get rid of them now; don't wait. Firing an employee might not be pleasant for you, but it's a necessary part of your job.

2. **Forming an Advisory Board:** An advisory board is made up of outside experts who informally counsel the company. This group differs from the board of directors in several ways, but most importantly the advisory board does not have fiduciary duties to the company and therefore has no legal liability. Advisors are usually chosen based on their connections within the industry, access to funding, or business acumen. Advisory boards typically meet four times a year, although it is not

uncommon for management to communicate with them more frequently. If you can compensate members of the advisory board in some way, you will most likely attract higher-quality participants who will be willing to dedicate more of their time, talent, and treasure to the success of the company.

3. *Talking Truth to Power:* As businesses grow, new layers of management are added, which can often hurt communication within the company. When customer service representatives and other lower level employees hear about problems, they frequently do not mention them to their bosses for fear of being blamed, fired, or assigned additional work. As a result, important information does not filter up to senior management where it could be handled. In some cases the problems are so serious that they can threaten the viability of the company itself. To prevent this from happening, management needs to promote the importance of communicating information, implementing systems ensuring smooth information flow, and rewarding line employees for bringing important information to management's attention.

4. *Avoid Hiring Friends and Family:* Mixing business with friends and family almost always results in botched friendships, painfully awkward family dynamics, and a company that isn't any better off. Business is best kept separate from family and friends. If you're having a problem trying to explain this to someone, just point them here and blame it on us. Better yet, buy them their own copy of the book.

5. ***Retaining Control:*** If you are like most entrepreneurs, one of the most important reasons why you set out on your own was to control your destiny. Yet somehow, many lose track of this. Control is not conferred by title alone; it is a function of ownership and contract. Many small businesses have fallen by the wayside over control issues and disagreements between owners. To avoid these issues, we recommend never splitting ownership 50/50 with a partner. You have to have at least 50.1% to ensure that someone is in control and has final decision-making authority. Second, draft a buy/sell agreement for partners and specify how the partnership will amicably end. This will be explained in detail in Chapter 6. If a partner becomes detrimental to the future of the business, this document will enable you to take back control. Lastly, when trading a stake in ownership for investment, make sure that you leave ample ownership reserves for future rounds of financing.

7.2 Execution – Doing It Right or Closing Your Doors

Execution is the implementation of the company's plan. It requires considerable time, energy, diligence and oversight Effective execution is not about following the plan as it is written, but knowing when and how to deviate from it.

As we talk to entrepreneurs, we find that the concept of "management" is very broad and, oftentimes, amorphous. In reality, management is important in all aspects of your business. You must manage the sales process, manage cash, manage people, manage information, manage customer relations… and everything else.

An excellent business plan with poor execution is worthless. However execution is one of the more difficult parts of building any business. The world doesn't unfold according to the plan. Product development most often doesn't fit within schedules, sales almost always take longer to close, and customers don't find the product as valuable as the sales and marketing materials say.

The three things you must know about effectively executing:

1. *Developing Milestones for Tactics and Tasks:* Milestones are jobs with specific due dates, an agreed upon budget (when applicable), and someone responsible for its completion. They are most effective with a short time frame. Milestones with longer time frames are at higher risk of having problems. Dividing larger objectives and periods of time into smaller and more manageable milestones is a good way to prevent issues as much as possible. Remember that tactics and tasks are the granular level of planning that lead up to objectives and ultimately goals.

2. *Ability to Make Decisions Quickly:* As previously mentioned, time is not an ally for the small business and new ventures. An important strength of a successful entrepreneur is the ability to seize opportunities and respond to issues quickly. Speed alone is not the key to success; it's the combination of a quick response and a well-conceived plan. While entrepreneurs are famous for going with their gut to make a decision, it's really not as undisciplined a process as it sounds. Where many successful entrepreneurs can make an important decision with only preliminary information, non-entrepreneurial companies tend as a rule to require extensive research before making a decision. If and when an entrepreneur is wrong, they frequently change directions quickly, whereas the non-entrepreneurial company usually has to study why it's not working and what went wrong.

3. *Identifying and Managing Key Business Metrics:*
Entrepreneurs have to identify which business statistics
are most important for managing the business successfully
and monitor those data sets daily. To help determine
what information is most important to your business, you
must consider what has to be accomplished to achieve
your plan. As previously discussed, the company's cash
position is always something you want to have at the tip
of your fingers. Additional information includes:

→ Aging of accounts receivable
→ Aging of accounts payable
→ Sales activity – number of calls made, number of
   qualified leads identified, number of proposals
   outstanding, length of time proposals have been
   outstanding, number of sales
→ Comparison of actual performance to budget
→ Compliance of vendors and customers with contracts
→ Compliance of business with matters such as
   payment of payroll taxes

The exact data sets will vary by industry; what's important is to
identify the critical information, put in systems to gather the
information, monitor the data regularly, set off alarms when there is a
problem and identify opportunities to make positive changes to the
business.

Conclusion

Many first time entrepreneurs spend just a little time thinking about
their business beyond the product. The product can subsume the
entrepreneur and become the be-all end-all of the venture. Through
a robust and creative plan, however, you've seen how much value can
be added to your product and company to drastically increase the
likelihood of success. Congratulations, your company and plan have
been fleshed out and now it's time to raise money for your venture.

CHAPTER 6:
One For the Money

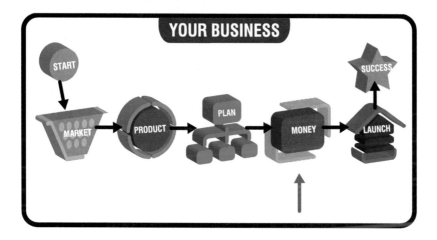

"Money is better than poverty, if only for financial reasons."
- Woody Allen, Comedian and Actor

"Plans are only good intentions unless they immediately
degenerate into hard work."
- Peter Drucker, Author and Management Guru

Objective

To demonstrate how to accurately project revenues and expenses,
build a business plan that can stand the heat of investors, and
ultimately raise money for your venture.

What You Need to Know About the Money

Everyone remembers the first time that they saw the space shuttle blast off: The clock at the Kennedy Space Center ticking backwards, the first puffs of smoke from the rocket boosters, and finally the ignition propelling the shuttle into the sky. This scene has universally captured our imagination for the past 40 years. On television, the whole experience may last just minutes, but the shuttle's launch is really the culmination of thousands of tasks performed by hundreds of people years prior to countdown. The clock actually begins ticking down from T minus 43 hours, about three days before liftoff, and NASA's pre-launch guidebook is a five volume manual that consists of more than 5,000 pages of instructions. These "last minute" preparations ensure a smooth and safe launch.

Fortunately, in business, the pre-launch step is much simpler, but no less important in determining whether your launch will be a success. Here is where you build your financial projections, perform our diagnostic test on what you've done thus far, write the business plan, and seek out funding. All of these steps are tied into the business model you have built. The point of each of these steps is to raise enough capital to start out on the right foot.

We believe that many dot-coms failed in the early 2000's because they didn't follow through on these steps. In their rush to get to market, they built poor business models based on flawed assumptions. They projected record sales and wrote lofty and ridiculous business plans. Many were given millions of dollars by goggle-eyed investors. Yet within a few months, the money had been spent and the business was a burned out cautionary tale. When the well runs dry, entrepreneurs are usually dumbfounded and blame their failure on anything but themselves – fickle investors, capital markets, etc. – while they should have been looking inward.

The truth is that it all comes back to the business model and any flawed assumptions. For example, Mortgage.com believed that its business was immune to economic cycles. The company did exceptionally well in its early years when interest rates were falling and homeowners were willing to refinance online, but when interest rates soared, fewer people were interested in refinancing. This effectively killed Mortgage.com because refinancing accounted for so much of its business.

Eric Wasserstrom, an analyst at UBS Warburg, said of the company, "Although [Mortgage.com] tried to get in on the business of originating mortgages, none worked. Home owners, especially first timers, wanted to sit across a desk from a lender so they could ask questions."[27] The company tried to adjust its business model, but with limited funds and already entrenched in this market, it couldn't do it.

Your projections and plan must be built on accurate and viable assumptions because they are the key to the funds you'll need to raise.

The Map to the Money

Step 8
Pre-Launch Steps

---

[27] Krantz, Matt. "What Detonated Dot-Bombs?." USA Today 04 Dec 2000:

Step 8: Pre-launch

8.1 Projections – Paint by Numbers

Financial projections should offer the best look into the business's crystal ball. How many units are you going to sell in the first three years and how much will that cost to produce? How much cash will you have? What will be your company's bottom line at the end of five years? Projections put the meat on the bones of the planning phase you just completed. The process forces you to sit down and instead of saying, "Sales will go through the roof once we launch," to come up with estimates of what those numbers could be.

The primary objectives for building financial projections are:

→ Determining how much cash you'll need to run the business
→ Validating the effectiveness of your tactics
→ Testing new assumptions

Developing projections requires time, patience, and attention to detail. To do this effectively, you have to fully understand what information you're trying to present and how to prove it. You can't just say that sales are going to grow 25% every year for the next five; you need evidence in which to base that growth rate which you can then extrapolate from.

First and foremost, projections are for you. They will inform your strategy and execution and give you a ruler by which to measure how your new company is doing. They are also important in attracting funding. In fact, many seasoned investors and advisors will skip over the wonderful prose in the business plan and go directly to the financial projections because for them projections indicate what's right and what's wrong.

As projections generally have an audience beyond the company, make sure that they are aesthetically pleasing. Even if your math is perfect and the numbers look great, you still have to put it all together in as attractive and professional a format as possible for your various audiences.

The Fallacy of Not Focusing on Revenues

When building financial projections, many new entrepreneurs err by spending the bulk of their time calculating expenses without adequately considering revenues. Most assume that revenues will just be there. Yet the overwhelming majority of a new venture's success depends on generating revenues, not managing expenses. Why then do so many new entrepreneurs blindly assume that their product will sell? These are just some of the fallacies we hear:

→ "Making sales is going to be easy; everybody we asked said that they think we've got a great idea."

→ "Our service makes so much sense people would be stupid not to buy it."

→ "I'm being extremely conservative. I'm assuming we're going to sell only 1% of our entire market in year 1, and 2.5% each year after. Now that's conservative."

These aren't rare exceptions. But the real reason that entrepreneurs often spend most of their time on costs is that they are much easier to project than revenues. Costs are more tangible – from the rent check you know that you'll have to sign to the salaries you'll have to pay out. Of course you're hopeful and confident in your product's ability to sell, but the process of projecting revenues and thinking about how you can actually sell 5,000 units this year will undoubtedly help you get there.

Roll Up Your Sleeves

Before we get started, we have to spend some time building financial projections. Ever your willing guide, here are a few pointers:

➜ Remember to devote the right amount of time to developing your revenue projections.

➜ The most common mistakes entrepreneurs make in building financial projections are issues relating to the timing of revenues, expenses and cash flows. Remember that having cash today is better than having cash tomorrow.

➜ Be careful when developing your assumptions. Don't over-reach. Ridiculous assumptions will lead to ridiculous projections. Assume wisely.

➜ You need to be comfortable working with an electronic spreadsheet like Microsoft Excel or Lotus 1-2-3. If you are not, please find someone to teach you.

Let Us Help You

At our website www.entrepreneurialdivide.com, we've built a template for your projections. As we have come up with the various categories of revenues and expenses, the process should be easier and cleaner on your end. Keep in mind that it is not perfect for you and your business. There is no one size that fits all template. However, it will be a very useful guide. To use the model at our website you will be asked to register for the site. Then, enter the code **03487-42784** where requested.

The Assumption Sheet

The assumption sheet describes how you build up to the numbers in your projections. You don't project revenues and expenses from thin air; instead they are based on assumptions that you make in order to gaze into the future. For example, while you don't know for sure that you could hire a manager for $5,000/ month, you assume this to be accurate based on your past experience and your understanding of the labor market, and thus base the line item "salary expenses" on this assumption.

The assumption sheet usually contains as few as 50 and as many as 250 assumptions. More assumptions usually indicates that you've divided each section in which there is a dollar impact on your business into the smallest element reasonably possible.

While you may be tempted to assume that you will sell your product to a certain percentage of the market each month, without examining each of the factors that will drive sales, these numbers are arbitrary and meaningless. Your sales numbers instead need to be based on your sales and marketing tactic assumptions as described in Chapter 5.

Often a company's sales are tied to its marketing effort and in developing your projections, you could use marketing dollars spent as a proxy for sales revenues. Here's the thought process: When direct mail is sent to prospects, some will respond. Of those who respond, you'll close sales with some of them. Based on that progression, you build your total sales estimate from direct marketing.

Your assumption sheet would include a line for direct mail in which you would put the number of pieces being sent each month, the cost per each direct mail piece and the response rate you expect (Fig. 6-1). Then add another line to indicate the percent of leads that you believe can be converted into sales calls. You would also have an assumption for the percent of sales calls you believe can be closed. With this information, include any direct sales related costs associated with making the sale call, such as travel and entertainment. Your assumption sheet will look like this:

Fig. 6-1

	Pieces Sent/Month	Cost/Mailer	Response Rate	Lag Time from Mailing
Direct Mail:	1,500	$0.75	2.3%	1 month

	% of Leads that Turn into Sales Calls	Travel & Entertainment per Average Sales Call	% of Sales Calls Closed	Lag Time from Call
Sales Factors:	33%	$100.00	5.0%	2 months

Average Sales Price

	Yr. 1	Yr. 2	Yr. 3	Annual Maintenance Fee
Product:	$7,500	$8,500	$9,500	15%

Completing your assumption sheet will require that you go through this exercise for every item that directly impacts revenue and costs. Through the magic of an electronic spreadsheet, each of these assumptions can now be easily updated as needed and the results quickly calculated throughout the spreadsheet.

To make this easier to read, it's common to divide your assumptions into categories from top to bottom, e.g., revenue assumptions, variable costs, fixed costs, financing-related costs, and tax-related costs. With your assumption sheet complete, you're ready to turn to the actual development of the projections.

The Month-By-Month and Year-By-Year Projections
Generally businesses project out either three or five years. In either case, the first year should be divided into months and the second year

by quarters. This reflects the fact that investors are more interested in your projections earlier on and want to see how you intend to spend their money from day one. Here is what your spreadsheet should look like:

Month 1 Month 2··Month 12 Total Yr. 1··Quarter 5 Quarter 6

Now, label the rows starting with the revenues. We recommend that you have line items for new units sold in each period, customer attrition, cumulative units sold (if that item is important in calculating revenue), and product price for that month. The bottom line, depending on the number of products you have, should be total revenues and look something like this:

	Month 1	Month 2	Month 3	•••
Total Revenues				
Number of New Customers				
Customers Deteriorating				
Cumulative # of Sales				
Average Product Price				
Total Revenues:				

After the revenue section, skip a couple of rows and enter your expense line items. Remember, expenses are calculated using the information in the assumption sheet, just like the revenue items above. In the expense area, it's best to divide expenses into variable costs and fixed costs:

→ **Variable costs** are any costs associated with the number of products produced and sold. Examples are the cost for the raw material(s) used in building each product, the cost of selling that product, any sales commission associated with the sale of that product, and so on. These costs are directly tied to sales volume.

➜ **Fixed costs** are any costs that a company will have to pay regardless of how many products are produced and sold. Examples are salaries and benefits, rent, phone lines, business insurance, accounting and legal, and so on. These costs are not related to sales volume.

	Month 1	Month 2	Month 3	• • •
Total Expenses				
Variable Expenses				
Cost of Goods Sold				
Travel & Entertainment				
Sales Commissions				
Legal and Accounting				
Shipping Costs				
Total Variable Expenses:				
Fixed Expenses				
Salaries and Benefits				
Rent				
Phone				
Supplies				
Insurance				
Miscellaneous				
Total Fixed Expenses:				
Total Expenses:				
Net Profit/(Loss)				
Depreciation				
Interest				
Taxes				
Net Profit After Tax				

With the spreadsheet setup, add your formulas into the spreadsheet for each cell. Your formulas pull into action all of the assumptions from your assumption sheet. **Double check every formula to make** sure you haven't made simple mistakes – a small error or missed decimal could cost you thousands of dollars! After entering all your formulas, you should have a fully-completed spreadsheet. Add another row (two lines below Net Profit after Tax) titled Cash Requirements and additional rows for any investment formulas you might want to include. Review your numbers to make sure everything looks reasonable. Now look at your results. Do projections deliver the type of returns you seek? This is your "Baseline Scenario."

"It amazes us how often people don't even look at their final numbers to check to see if they are realistic. Here's a hint: If your revenues in year 3 are starting to look like the Gross National Product of France, there are mistakes in your projections. We guarantee it."

Charlie

Alternative Scenarios

You are almost done. Using financial statements to project the future is as much art as it is science. To get a more complete picture, consider the business' projected performance through two other lenses: a conservative scenario and an optimistic scenario. The way to do this is by manipulating your assumption sheet. To show a more conservative scenario, pull back on assumptions and assume you'll sell less or materials will cost more. Conversely, for the potential scenario, increase your original key revenue drivers to account for things going somewhat better than your baseline scenario projects. Make sure you highlight and justify the key drivers that you adjusted to reach the various scenarios.

Go back and study your results. Are there certain tactics that are not delivering the results you expected? If so, this is the time to make any last minute changes to your tactics before you run your business through our New Venture Test Model, which we will discuss next.

"Caution! Don't label your alternative scenarios 'best case' and 'worst case'. It can always be better and it can definitely always be worse."

Charlie

Finally, for each of your three scenarios, develop a balance sheet, cash flow statement, and profit and loss statement for each year in your projections. Because turning financial projections into financial statements is a full business school course, we won't fully get into that here. Instead, we encourage you to look at our projections template at www.entrepreneurialdivide.com, which helps you to turn projections into financial statements.

If you're not comfortable building your financial projections or want to learn more about it, we recommend that you check out the following books: Building Financial Models with Microsoft Excel: A Guide for Business Professionals by K. Scott Proctor and Building Financial Models by John Tjia.

8.2 New Venture Test – Test Driving Your Business
Over the years, we have developed our own proprietary "New Venture Test Model" to help us determine whether or not to invest in a new business. We have put this model to use to predict the probability of a new venture's success and pinpoint problematic areas. The model has proven to be quite accurate predicting success and failure.

Knowing precisely where and how big the problems are, as told through the model, we can quickly decide to pass on the investment opportunity or develop a targeted strategy to overcome these challenges.

To help you develop a realistic sense of your company's chances, we are offering our model to you. This comprehensive tool uses 100+ variables in determining a company's strengths and weaknesses. To use this free model *for a limited time*, go to the book's website at www.entrepreneurialdivide.com. Once you registered, you will be asked for the code number, type in the code number: **03487-42784** where designated.

Once registered, proceed through the model by answering the questions regarding your business as accurately and honestly as you can. If you're not sure how to answer a particular question, default toward the conservative to get the more accurate picture.

The model will automatically calculate a score that indicates a probability of success based on your inputs. Don't be overly alarmed if the first time you run your business through the model you come out with a low score. Most first time entrepreneurs do. This is where the model really excels; it will highlight the areas in your business where you're weakest. These areas are where you need to focus your attention. Take time and look at the results closely. Now remember, there is no way to absolutely predict success for every situation.. The goal of the model is to force you to look at your proposed business or investment in a comprehensive way, to show you how all of these factors work together, and to show you areas that need a lot more attention.

8.3 Business Plan – Writing It All Down

You might be a bit perplexed with all the different terminology related to planning. Chapter 5 largely focused on planning, so it's a fair question to ask why the business plan itself is in this chapter. In Chapter 5, we discussed strategic planning as an essential process in a new business. These are the steps you had to go through to get your product and company ready for action. The business plan, on the other hand, is an object. It is a physical document that expresses to the world what your business is and how it works – the natural result of planning, including the strategic planning described in Chapter 5. The business plan itself, however, is the most important thing that you can create in order to raise money for your business.

You should – no, you must – create some type of a business plan before you are ready to start your business. This plan shows how you intend to conduct your business, from soup to nuts.

Before we get into more detail, we should tell you that we are often asked how long a business plan should be. We'd like to be able to say that your business plan should be between X and Y pages long, but there is no magic formula. There are two good ways to determine length, however. First, does the business plan include all of the things you'd like to see if you were considering an investment in the company? Second, get a trusted friend with business expertise to review the plan, and to offer honest constructive criticism. The size of the business plan is, in part, also based on the type of business you are forming, your short-term goals, and the audience for whom you are writing. As such, your business plan should be custom-tailored to your own circumstances.

In addition, your business plan should be treated as a "living document". By that we mean that you shouldn't just write the plan, stick it in a drawer and never look at it again. As your business changes, your plan needs to be updated accordingly.

Let's now look at how to prepare a successful business plan:

1) **The Why and the Wherefore – Determine Your Plan's Objectives and Audience**

   The reasons you are writing a business plan and the audience for that plan will determine the scope and content. The most typical reasons for preparing a plan and the structure/content differences that may arise are:

   → *Cash:* Business plans are the single most important document that you will give to potential funders. The differences in how you write the plan are related to the type of funder you are approaching:

   - *Professional Investors:* The business plan for professional investors (like venture capital firms) will need to be the most comprehensive. An investor will require a full picture of the business before making an investment decision and your business plan is the vehicle for painting this picture.

   - *Friends and Family:* Asking for money is a great way to find out who your friends really are and whether Aunt Susie really believes that you are her favorite. Typically friends and family only want to see the Executive Summary, which we'll talk more about later. They are probably more concerned about your character and how they will get their money back than your EBITDA at the end of your second fiscal year.

   - *Lenders:* If your business is at a point where it can borrow from institutional lenders like a bank, your plan will need to focus more on financial information and company assets available to secure the loan, and less on the inner-workings of the company. This will vary by lender.

- *Management:* A business plan is a great way to keep management focused. Since it will contain objectives, goals, and tactics, it's valuable to share with the firm's management. At the same time, though, you will probably not want to give out the entire plan since there is information that you might not want to share such as your salary.

- *Potential Board Members:* You should have a board of directors or advisory board for reasons we discussed in Chapter 5. If you are recruiting talented people, they will want to know as much as they can about the business – including your more confidential information – before agreeing to serve on the board.

→ *Roadmap:* When you start a new business, there are many things going on at the same time. A business plan can be the basis on which you move forward with your business and keep the company focused and on task.

→ *Your company's goals, objectives and tactics:* Just putting these thoughts into words will increase the company's focus and flesh out how you intend to get from point A to point B.

→ *Financial projections.* As we discussed earlier in this chapter, financial projections are an absolute necessity. A business plan enables you to put the financial projections in the context of how you will execute.

→ *Individual responsibilities and monitoring performance.* A good business plan will set forth not only the goals, but also the milestones you need in place to enable you to measure success. It is likely that portions of your plan will be a useful tool for reinforcing to employees what is expected of them and the milestones they need to reach in order to be successful.

2) Structure and Contents of the Business Plan

There is, without a doubt, a somewhat "standard" form that business plans take. You can find templates on the Internet or buy a software package that will help you generate a plan. But all business plans are different. As you construct your business plan, make sure that your plan includes similar sections to the following example (and, for many of the sections, we've added detail for you to consider).

Example:

> *The company, Superior Medical Solutions, Inc. (SMS) has developed a revolutionary way to process, disinfect and dispose medical waste such as needles, blades, scalpels and other sharps. The product is a small machine that fits on the wall of a surgical suite, hospital room or physician's examination room. Through a patented process, the device exposes the waste to incredibly high temperatures to reduce the volume by 98% and then subjects the processed waste to ultraviolet light to kill germs and bacteria.*

1. First Impression – The Cover Page:

Your plan should be neatly bound and have a cover page with the name of your business, the date of the plan and your contact information. The cover page should also have, at the bottom, a legend saying that it is "Confidential and Proprietary". These words should also appear in the footer at the bottom of each page of the plan.

2. **First Impact – The Executive Summary:**
   The executive summary is the most important part of the business plan. This is the overview of the problem and your solution and may be the only part of the plan read by certain audiences – especially when dealing with friends and family who don't care as much about the inner workings of the business or with professional investors who will use the executive summary to determine whether they want to have any serious follow-up discussion with you.

   → **The Hook:** Make sure you start with a powerful first sentence. You've got one chance to hook the reader.

   > SMS would talk about why medical waste disposal is a huge and growing problem, who has needs (like hospitals and doctors offices) and why the system increases safety in disposing of medical waste.

   → Validate Why You Should Exist: What is your reason for being? We addressed this in detail in Chapter 4, Step 3.1. If you can't explain this clearly and succinctly, you don't really have a business. In addition to setting forth your reason for being, your validation section should also:
   - Emphasize your strengths
   - Describe your competitive advantages
   - Describe any patents, copyrights, or contracts that gives you business a leg up
   - Explain the strength of the company's management
   - Describe any unique industry expertise or connections

   → **How Long is Too Long:** Conventional wisdom is to keep the executive summary to $1^{1/2}$ to four pages. Don't get too hung up on length because you need to be thorough in your presentation; however, if you go beyond five pages it no longer feels like a "summary."

3. **Our Sandbox Is The Biggest In Town – Describe The Market Opportunity:**

By now you've learned the importance of identifying the market and understanding your prospects' needs, wants, and priorities. Therefore, it should be obvious that describing this is an absolutely vital part of your business plan. Make sure you:

→ Identify needs
→ Quantify needs
→ Describe the size of the market opportunity
→ Describe the value proposition (as we've defined it)
→ Describe your product concept
→ Explain how your product satisfies these needs
→ Identify prospects
→ Explain the rationale for why prospects should buy your product
→ Identify your competitors

> *In the medical waste industry, the needs are protecting nurses and other healthcare workers from needle sticks and other exposures. There were more than 1 million accidental needle sticks last year with an associated cost of more than $6 billion to test and treat them. Further, there are 1.1 million hospital rooms, 926,000 nursing home rooms, and 1.45 million physician exam rooms in the country.*

4. **Who is Playing in Your Sandbox – Industry Overview and Competition:**

Describe the industry in which you will be doing business. This requires more than the market opportunity, which you will have covered already. This is a discussion of the players, trends and competitors.

> *The Zapper destroys waste and turns it into a substance that can be disposed of with ordinary garbage. This is a better solution than burning waste which uses a lot of energy and increases air pollution.*

5. **What Your Future Holds – Your Business Model:**
    Describe your business model clearly. Once again, a good business model explains how a company plans to leverage its advantages, in view of its strategies, to deliver maximum net value to prospects, thereby maximizing your company's value. Please refer back to Chapter 5 where we presented a detailed discussion of business models.

> *SMS will give hospitals 2 units to try, one for the emergency room and one for a patient room for 30 days at no cost. In addition, SMS will provide free on-site training.*

6. **What Your Future Looks Like – Business Strategy:**
    Explain, in detail, what you are going to do to make your company successful. This is where you put into writing what you developed in Chapter 5. This requires that you address matters such as:

    → *Goals:* Goals are what you hope to achieve with your business in the next 3 to 5 years.

    → *Objectives:* Objectives are created to achieve goals. Since goals tend to be long-term, they are extremely difficult to manage, whereas objectives are shorter-term and therefore easier to deal with.

    → *Tactics:* Tactics are the actions you will take to achieve your objectives. We like to think of these as the actions "in the trenches." You will need to have tactics that address each area of your business, and here are some examples:

- *Sales and Marketing:*
  - o What process will you use and what software will you use, for sales management?
  - o How do you plan to reach customers?
  - o Will you require a unique marketing strategy for each product or can you leverage a single marketing strategy?
  - o How much of your budget will you spend on sales and marketing?
  - o What strategic alliances and partners will you pursue?
  - o What marketing tools will you use? Will you use TV, direct mail, brochures, customer lists, mailers, letters, or PR, catalogs, Internet, or tradeshows?

- *Pricing:*
  - o How will you price your product?
  - o Will there be one price or will you segment the market by price?

- *Distribution:*
  - o Will you have your own distribution system?
  - o Will you engage a company with more access to your customers to distribute your product?
  - o Who will be responsible for managing inventory?

- *Growth:*
  - o How will you grow initially?
  - o Where will future growth come from?
  - o Are there cross-sell opportunities?
  - o Can you raise prices?
  - o How big do you want to be in 5 years?

- *Organization and Management:*
  - o Company background

- o Company vision
- o Company mission
- o Management team

- *Operations:*
  - o What is your implementation and execution schedule?
  - o What are your implementation and execution issues (actual and potential)?
  - o What systems, programs and tools are required (e.g., do you need to license necessary software)?
  - o What are the key metrics and milestones?
  - o What are your logistics plans?
  - o Are there other assets such as patents, copyrights, or valuable contracts?
  - o Where is funding coming from?
  - o Are there any other operational issues you believe need to be addressed?

7. **Showing You Can Make Money – Financial Projections:**
No business plan is complete or credible without financial projections. These will showcase the results you are working to achieve. As we covered in detail in the first section of this chapter, financial projections include (i) assumptions; (ii) the actual projections based on the assumptions; (iii) Profit and Loss Statement; (iv) Statement of Cash Flows; and (v) Balance Sheet. In addition, you need to show key financial metrics such as:

→ Breakeven point
→ Investor payback
→ Return on investment (ROI)
→ Internal rate of return (IRR)
→ Net present value (NPV)

8. **What's In It For the Investor – Exit Strategy:**
   If you are getting money from an investor, you have to address the investor's exit strategy. How will they be able to cash out and what will be their return on investment? Do not leave this for the investor to try to figure out. You need to be upfront and honest about the way you calculate the ROI and what the ROI will be based on. This also requires that you clearly disclose all assumptions used in determining the exit valuation and the valuation methodology.

   Answering this question also requires that you lay out for the investor:

   → Current ownership
   → Where current funding came from
   → How much equity you are selling
   → Ownership following investment

   > *The most likely exit strategy for investors in SMS will be an acquisition of the company by a major medical products manufacturer. Public companies in the medical waste disposal market currently have an average price to earnings ratio of 22.5. A sale of the company 4 years from today at a valuation of $20 million will result in a 40%IRR for the investor.*

9. **It's A Jungle Out There – Risk Factors:**
   This is an important section and it is often overlooked in preparing a business plan. Your reader will know that there are risks to the investment; some will be obvious and some will not. If you don't address these, readers might assume you're out to lunch and you'll lose credibility. Risks, per se, are not show stoppers; the key is to make clear that you recognize the risks and to show how you plan to mitigate them. Be honest and forthcoming.

> *For SMS, material risks include losing FDA approval, challenges to our patent and access to specialized materials.*

10. The Big Finish – Conclusion:

At the end of the business plan, put in a few sentences summing up why this is a great business opportunity. Make sure this is brief and very powerful.

11. Extra Credit – Appendices:

Your business plan must be readable. What this means is that it needs to tell a story that is not unnecessarily dense. One way to give readers what they want, without breaking the flow, is to put certain information into appendices to the plan (and you can put summary information in the body of the plan). In our experience, the following items belong best in appendices:

→ Detailed financial projections: Your business plan will contain detailed summary financial data, but the full-blown financial projections (i.e., spreadsheets) can be in an appendix
→ Examples of brochures and marketing materials
→ Example of web pages
→ Copies of patents
→ Client/reference lists
→ Relevant secondary research reports
→ Press releases/news stories
→ Additional Market Data – Surveys

12. Keep It Quiet – Non-Disclosure Agreements (NDAs):

We are often asked if the entrepreneur should, when handing out the business plan, get an NDA signed. An NDA is an agreement between you and the recipient of the plan by which the recipient agrees to hold all of the information in the plan in strict confidence. As with so many situations, there is no clear cut answer. In general, we think it is a good idea to get an NDA. But, there will be exceptions:

→ Would you feel comfortable asking Uncle Bob to sign an NDA if he is kind enough to consider giving you money?

→ Many venture capitalists will not, as a policy, sign an NDA for many reasons. The most common is that they see so many business plans that they refuse to be burdened with trying to keep track of what they can, and what they can't, talk about.

Tricks for Improving Your Business Plan:

→ **Tell a Story.** As we discussed in Chapter 5, the story is an excellent marketing tool and it is also a great way to present your company in a business plan.

→ **Advocate for Your Business.** Don't be shy. Tell the reader why your business is great and why it will be a huge success. If that doesn't come through to the reader, then the reaction to your business will be lukewarm at best.

→ **Answer All Questions.** You will be doing your reader a real service, and your plan will have a greater impact, if you anticipate questions that the reader will have and answer them in the business plan.

→ **Document Your Findings.** If you make claims about things like market size and competitor's size, or if you use surveys to conduct market research, make sure you document your findings. Without clear authority for the statements, you will lose credibility.

➜ **Make Your Plan Easy to Read. Be kind to your reader.** If you are presenting a plan to an institutional investor, you can be assured that she has a lot of business plans to read. So, make your plan more readable by using section headings, underlining, bold, italics and highlighting as necessary. Don't go crazy though – if everything in the plan is highlighted, for example, then nothing looks special.

➜ **Use Diagrams, Charts, Pictures and Graphs.** Admit it – you like to look at pictures. The readers of your plan like to look at pictures, too. So, where logical, use diagrams, charts, pictures and graphs. Not only are they a great way to present summary information or numbers in a clear fashion, they break up the narrative.

➜ **Don't be Repetitive, Don't be Repetitive.** Seriously, don't be repetitive. Why? Admittedly, some repetition of information is necessary, but be careful. If you are continually repetitive, there can be only two outcomes, both of which are bad. First, you'll aggravate your reader. It makes the reader feel like you believe he is dumb and you have to keep repeating yourself to get the information through his thick skull. Second, you stand a very good chance of being inaccurate if you are repeating numbers.

Michael

"Charlie and I are always looking to invest in businesses and together we review a lot of business plans. Unfortunately for us, so many entrepreneurs must think that investors have periodic amnesia, considering they say the same thing over and over and over again. Believe me; we have never seen one paragraph so brilliant that it bears repeating five times."

Charlie

"We have seen more poorly written business plans than we care to remember. Some forget to include information on their backgrounds, others misspell common words, many leave off page numbers, most included financial projections that required a microscope to read; two even forget to include their contact information and name."

→ **Check Grammar and Spelling.** Proofread your business plan. It is so annoying to see errors like misspelled words; this suggests that you didn't care enough to, at the least, run spellchecker – but remember there are words spellchecker misses, too. In reality, once you've written, edited, and read your plan a number of times it gets harder and harder to spot errors. You need to find a good proofreader to help you.

→ **Number Pages and Use a Table of Contents.** Make it easy for the reader to find things in the plan.

Writing the business plan is a laborious task, but the payoff from a very good business plan is much higher than from a fair business plan.

8.4 Financing – Money Makes the World Go Round

News flash: You need money to run your business. We know you already knew that. The issue is not recognizing the need; the issue is finding the money. While money doesn't grow on trees, it can come from a number of places. Before we address the most common sources, here are some basic definitions:

→ **Debt** refers to borrowed money. It can come in the form of credit cards, where you owe money back to the credit card lender, or a loan where you agree to repay to the lender the money you borrow plus interest.

→ **Equity** refers to an ownership share of the business. In this case, the equity holder does not receive interest like on a loan.

With that by way of introduction, let's take a look at these various types of funding:

Fig. 6-2

Debt

	Secured	Avg. Rate	Avg. $ Amount	Difficulty of Getting
Credit Cards	No	12%-21%	$1,500 - $50,000	Easiest
Commercial Loan	Yes	1 - 3 + Prime	$5,000 - $1,000,000+	Adequate security is key
Home Equity & 2nd Mortgage	Yes	Prime to 2+	Related to equity in house	Relatively easy
Trade Credit	Not Usually	0% - 12%	Depending on vendor	30 – 60 days easy > 90 days difficult
A/R Financing	Yes	1 – 2 + Prime	Related to Amount of Receivables	Relatively easy
Factoring	Yes	20% - 30%	No limit if security is there	Relatively easy with security

Equity

Friends & Family	No	N/A	$1,000 – $250,000	Easiest of equity
Angel Investors	No	N/A	$25,000 – $500,000	Tied to building relationship
Venture Capital	Usually	Prime	$1,500,000 – $25,000,000+	Very small percent get funded
Strategic Alliances	No	N/A	Varies	Difficult

More Equity Considerations:

→ In determining whether to accept an equity investment or not, understand that a smaller piece of a larger pie may be worth much more than a larger piece of a smaller pie.

→ Be very comfortable with the growth and profitability you're projecting.

→ Pay particularly attention to any control you may be losing or could lose in the future. In many cases this becomes more important than the actual percent ownership.

→ Make sure you trust and can work closely with the investors and that you trust them.

Presenting To Potential Investors:

→ When deciding who from your company should be part of the presentation, involve as many members of the management team as possible.

→ You probably will only have about an hour; therefore, it's imperative that you keep the presentation on track.

→ Don't let the prospective investor's questions slow you down; ask them if it is acceptable for you to answer all questions at the end of the presentation.

→ For your presentation, consider addressing the following topics:

- Company history
- Problem / solution
- Market opportunity / size

- Customer benefits
- What's unique about your company or solution
- Market strategy
- Management team
- Competition
- Product & pricing strategy
- Financials / proposed transaction
- Liquidity strategy / IRR & payback

Here are a few final things to keep in mind:

1. Don't submit a business plan to a venture capital firm if you don't have a contact first. Think about it. VCs get a huge number of plans. The best way to have yours stand out is to have someone introduce you to the firm. Introductions can come from accountants, lawyers, other businessmen in the community with connections, etc.

2. Don't expect additional equity (i.e., equity beyond friends and family) if you haven't established some credibility with customers, most likely through beta testing.

3. You must be very clear and thorough in describing the market and your competitors.

4. Be clear about what the company does. If you have a complicated product, figure out a way to give a very clear explanation, probably with pictures.

5. Don't present unreasonable projections. If you do, you will quickly lose credibility.

Conclusion

Raising money for your business is a stressful, pride-swallowing endeavor. You may have to go door-to-door for several months to find an investor whose goals align closely with yours and with whom you believe a relationship is possible. A lot of trial and error goes with this process, but being prepared with realistic projections and a well thought out business plan, in addition to proving your business through our rigorous test will give you a significant advantage that others won't have when pounding the pavement in search of cash.

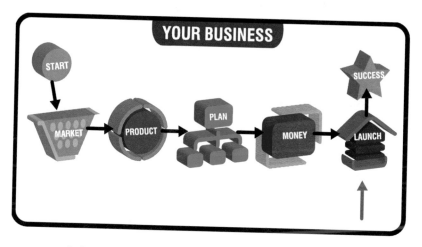

"The secret of getting ahead is getting started."
- Mark Twain, Writer and Entrepreneur

"Baseball is the only field of endeavor where a man can succeed
three times out of ten and be considered a good performer."
- Ted Williams, Major League Baseball All-Star

Objective
To help you make the most out of your cash, minimize the start-up
headaches, and avoid the common pitfalls in opening your doors
for business.

The launch of the business is that sacred entrepreneurial moment when you fling open your doors for the first time. Take a moment and relish the fact that you've made it this far. We know that you're excited and itching to get started, so don't dawdle; it's go time. Many entrepreneurs wrongfully assume that the launch is the finish line – and after making it through the market, product design and development, and planning hurdles, it's just smooth sailing. Surprisingly, however, this is an area where new entrepreneurs tend to make fatal errors. To ensure that you get off on the right foot, we'll show where most go wrong and how to avoid those traps – from forming the right kind of legal entity to tips on furnishing an office.

"Shit Happens!"

You may think that you crossed all of the "t's" and dotted each of the "i's," but there will always be problems that you never could have imagined which will challenge you and the business. This is as sure as a law of nature. Bet on gravity, principles of thermodynamics, and "shit happening" to your business when you launch. First time entrepreneurs generally share a rosy view of the world and either don't want to hear that there might be troubles lurking around the corner or believe that their business is immune to such issues. No doubt, this entrepreneurial optimism is important fuel for a new business, but first-timers often need a strong dose of realism to avoid some ugly situations. It's certainly possible that things will go perfectly according to plan, but we wouldn't bet on it. Shit happens. Preparing is just being smart.

Here are some examples of the things that can (and often do) happen in new ventures:

→ A major disagreement with your partner/s jeopardizes the relationship
→ A disgruntled employee threatens to sue you if you fire him

→ An employee quits and sells everything he learned at your company, goes to a direct competitor

→ Customers refuse to pay

→ Employees steal from you

Managing Risk

Entrepreneurs push the envelope by creating products that the world has not yet seen and by constantly challenging the status quo. This is what makes entrepreneurs succeed, but there's also a flipside to being a revolutionary. An innovative nature and speed to market typical in a new business can put entrepreneurs at risk if something goes wrong. And – as we already told you – something will always go wrong.

Just look at the big guys. Huge companies that spend millions of dollars on R&D and product testing often find themselves in deep trouble. In one of the largest recalls in the history of the U.S. electronics industry, Dell and Sony recalled millions of laptop computer batteries after they found that PCs were overheating and bursting into flames in 2006.[28] Mattel recently recalled over 20 million toys worldwide after their Chinese-made toys were found to have lead in them.[29]

How can a small business on a shoestring budget get things right the first time if the Fortune 500 behemoths can't? Just thinking about each of the worst-case scenarios in your own business might make you want to hide under the covers and close up shop. But you knew there would be risk. There's no way to get around it, but there are many things entrepreneurs can do to minimize and manage risk, ultimately protecting your personal assets and business.

---

[28] Darlin, Damon. Dell Recalls Batteries Because of Fire Threat." New York Times 14 Aug 2006

[29] http://money.cnn.com/2007/08/14/news/companies/mattel/index.htm?postversion=2007081409

Cash Is As Good As Money

As we previously mentioned, cash shortages are one of the primary reasons why most businesses fail. Remember that cash and profits are two very different things. Profit is a line on a financial statement that indicates how much revenue you brought in above expenses. Profit does not mean that you have money in your pocket. Cash does. Cash enables you to pay bills, buy stuff, and ultimately make your business run.

Most startups begin on a short leash and a tight budget, so what's really important is how good you are at turning minimal dollars into maximal output. You can judge how successful an entrepreneur will be by looking at how they spend their money. If they squander precious cash on rent in a fancy penthouse office in a posh part of town and treat themselves to a fancy steakhouse on the company's tab three times a week, it's safe to bet two things:

1. The vast majority of funding didn't come from their own wallet
2. They're not likely to be around for long

Anecdotal evidence suggests that the more money an entrepreneur is given upfront, the less likely they are to succeed. A case in point was the Internet boom. There seemed to be a direct correlation between how quickly a new venture bought a private plane and how fast their business went under. A coincidence? We think not.

This chapter goes into the often over-looked, common places where entrepreneurs can save a buck and ultimately earn a buck for their business. This is not a lesson in frugality so much as it is a guide to smart buying. These concepts have enabled the savviest entrepreneurs to stretch out their cash while their extravagant counterparts have long been out of business.

The Map to the Launch

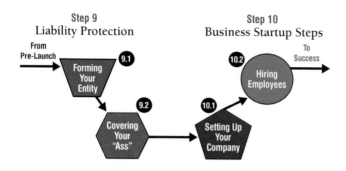

Step 9: Liability Protection

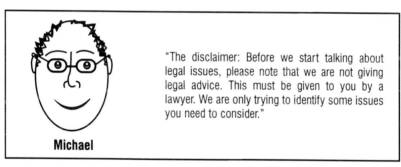

Michael

"The disclaimer: Before we start talking about legal issues, please note that we are not giving legal advice. This must be given to you by a lawyer. We are only trying to identify some issues you need to consider."

Charlie

"Good grief! Once a lawyer, always a lawyer."

9.1 Forming an Entity – Pass the Cigars

The biggest practical risk some entrepreneurs run into is that they get so excited about actually starting their business that they put off what they perceive to be the less exciting aspects of the process. They decide that their time and money is better spent on operational matters and away from what they assume to be the comparatively dull legal and risk-management issues. Their mistake is like a giant "Kick me" sign on the company's back because deferring these issues leads to higher risk and complications down the road. So instead, start off the right way. Remember: It is much easier to implement the right structure and risk-management programs at the outset than to go back and to try fixing things once they go awry.

One of the early steps is to decide the form in which you will conduct your business. The primary reason for this is to protect you from the liabilities of the business. This is like a kind of insurance. If you form a separate legal entity and operate it properly, you can effectively insulate yourself and your personal assets from most company liability. Operating as a sole proprietorship does not provide any protection from liability, so we are not going to spend any time talking about it.

While legal entities afford varying degrees of liability protection, there are certain classes of liabilities that no legal entity can protect against, such as guarantees, certain taxes owed to the government, and certain types of fraud. A personal guarantee is a contract where an individual or corporation agrees to be responsible for any obligations owed by the company in the case that the company party defaults on its debts. You're thinking: I'd be completely naked. Why would I sign this? The reality is you'll probably have little choice. It's unlikely that that any landlord or bank will lease you property or lend you money without requiring you to put your signature on the personal guarantee line.

To help you determine which legal entity is best for your company, review the summary chart below. The most common alternatives are a corporation, a limited liability company (LLC), and a limited partnership.

Fig. 7-1

Entity Type:	Corporation	LLC	Limited Partnersip
Formation	Rules for formation vary from state to state. Generally involves reserving a name and filing Articles of Incorporation with the Secretary of State.	Rules for formation vary from state to state. Generally involves reserving a name and filing Articles of Organization with the Secretary of State.	Formation rules vary from state to state. Involves reserving a name and filing Certificate of Limited Partnership with the Secretary of State.
Ownership	Can be owned by 1 or more shareholders. Shareholders can enter into a shareholders agreement to deal with operating and co-ownership issues.	Can be owned by 1 or more members. Members enter into an operating agreement to deal with operating and ownership issues.	Must have a general partner and a limited partner. Partners can enter into partnership agreements to deal with operating and co-ownership issues.
Liability	Shareholders will be protected from the debts and liabilities of the business so long as they follow basic rules.	Members will be protected from the debts and liabilities of the business so long as they follow basic rules.	The general partner has unlimited liability for the liabilities of the business; the limited partner is protected from these liabilities.
Taxes	Generally, corporations are taxpayers; they pay tax on their income and shareholders pay tax on dividend distributions. A corporation can, under certain circumstances, elect to be treated as an S corporation which means the S corporation which makes it a pass-though entity (see LLC). There are limitations on number and type of shareholders.	A limited liability company is a pass-through entity, meaning that the LLC is not a taxpayer; rather, it reports its income, losses, etc. and each member claims his share of the LLC's tax items on his personal income tax return.	A limited partnership is a pass-through entity.
Other	More rule driven and less flexible than an LLC	Most flexible of the entities	Has no real benefit over an LLC

To summarize the chart:

Ease of Use: Corporation laws tend to be very prescriptive, meaning that they set out rules for what the corporation can and can't do in terms of shareholder relationships, allowable provisions in bylaws, etc. On the other hand, LLC laws are more flexible, allowing the members to agree amongst themselves about almost all aspects of their relationship.

→ *Taxes:* Every time a new session of Congress opens, the same battle cry is heard once again: "No more double taxation!" This is the current policy of taxing a certain company's profits twice. First, the company is required to pay taxes on its profit, and second, when that profit is distributed to the owners, it is taxed once again. S corporations, partnerships, sole proprietorships and LLCs are not considered separate entities and therefore are not double taxed. However, C corporations are double taxed. While no company wants to be double taxed, C corporations are best for big companies. S corporations and LLCs have limits to the number of shareholders they can have; C corporations have fewer such limitations.

→ *Liability Issues:* Almost all of these legal entities provide some kind of liability protection to the owners of the business. The one exception is the sole proprietorship which offers no liability protection. To maintain a liability shield, a company must, among other things, remain in "good standing" with the state agency governing business entities and be treated as an entity separate from the owners (i.e., use company stationery, use business cards, don't pay personal expenses out of the corporation unless they are shown as loans on the company books).

The Process for Forming Your Entity

While this process might vary from state to state, the basic steps include:

→ Reserving a name
→ Filing articles of incorporation or articles of organization in your state
→ Obtaining a federal taxpayer identification number from the IRS
→ Obtaining identification numbers from your state (as required)

Thanks to the Internet, forming an entity has gotten a whole lot easier. Now many of the steps in the process can be done by going to both your individual state's Secretary of State website and using the IRS website (www.irs.gov).

9.2 Covering Your Ass – Protecting Yourself

Despite the fact that your legal entity will provide some liability protection, it is not sufficient. There are several other risk-minimizing precautions both through contracts and various kinds of insurance that help shield you and your company.

Charlie

"You know, there might just be an opportunity here: With so much 'ass covering' going in at big businesses, there's got to be some type of product we could develop. How about a "Cover Your Ass" Insurance Policy whereby holders of such insurance who can prove they took the requisite steps to cover their ass would get compensated if they lose their job."

Contracts and Insurance Worthy of Consideration

Because of the complexity of legal documents for business, the following information is intended to be a primer on the topic, not an exhaustive list. You are encouraged to seek out legal advice to determine the best course of action, particularly when the stakes are high.

In our own work, a few common agreements and insurance policies have come in handy over and over again.

Agreements Between the Co-Owners

Many new businesses are started by more than one person and those partners need to agree on certain terms as early on as possible. Even if you're going into business with your college roommate or twin sibling, this is still a good idea. Partner disputes are not prevented by initial good intentions. Therefore, at the outset of any business relationship, partners should discuss "what if" situations, develop contingencies, and plan ahead to avoid them. The further you get down the road, the busier you will be and the less important this type of contract will seem. Don't make that mistake. Make a co-owner agreement a priority. As you structure the agreement, consider these issues:

→ *Effort:* You may both be willing to work hard today, but what happens when one of you doesn't want to work as hard as the other. How do you measure hard work?

→ *Governance of your business:* Governance, in comparison with management, relates to setting the overall policy for the firm. It specifies how the big decisions that steer the company will be made. Is there a board of directors? If there are two equal partners, what happens if they deadlock on an issue? If there are three or more equal partners, what voting outcome is necessary to approve an issue? If they are unequal partners, what vote is necessary?

→ **Management of your business:** This is the day-to-day running of the business. What titles will the partners hold? Will one partner be "first among equals"? Is the division of labor clear so that each partner fully understands the aspects of the business over which each is responsible?

→ **Delegation of management:** Often entrepreneurs want to do it all (and believe they can) not knowing how to share responsibility with others in the firm. There simply aren't enough hours in the day for this. Can you delegate?

→ **Disability of a partner (short term / long term):** What will the business do if the disabled partner is an essential player on a day to day basis? You went into business relying on each to pull his weight, but unforeseeable setbacks can quickly alter your reality.

→ **Death of a partner:** What will the business do if one of the partners dies? Will one partner end up in business with the spouse or heir of the other partner?

→ **Dispute resolution:** If you do end up in a dispute, how will it be resolved? Do you want to consider mediation and/or arbitration?

When issues surface and contingencies have been established, typical problems might find easy solutions. However, in some cases, divorce may be the only viable option for partners. In this case, how do you determine who has to relinquish their claim and how do you value shares and their restitution? If you address this in the co-owner agreement we've been discussing, things will go more smoothly.

Non-Competes, Non-Solicit, Confidentiality and Non-Disclosures

Depending on the type of business you have, you may want your employees to sign restrictive covenant agreements. These agreements protect the business and any proprietary knowledge and competencies, giving the employer certain guarantees if an employee leaves the firm.

→ *Covenants not to compete* seek to prevent the former employee from becoming a head-to-head competitor. Employers can spend a lot of time and money training employees and sharing proprietary information and insights. The employer does so with the expectation that the employee will not pick up and open a competitive business across the street.

→ *Covenants not to solicit* are somewhat like a covenant not to compete but focus specifically on the firm's customers. These agreements prevent former employees from stealing customers from the firm.

→ *Covenants not to induce or hire away employees* seeks to prevent the former employee from raiding the firm and hiring away all the good people. The former employee may have had access to payroll information and would, therefore, know how much extra to offer employees to leave. In such a situation, the employer again loses the benefit of time and money it has invested in training employees.

→ *Confidentiality and non-disclosure agreements* seek to protect trade secrets and other confidential information that have value to the employer. Trade secrets, generally, include proprietary business methods, plans, formulas, and methods. Many states have laws that specifically define what constitutes a trade secret, as with Coca-Cola's secret formula. Confidential information, while not a secret formula written down somewhere, includes things like customers lists, which are no less important for a company to protect.

Insurance

One thing you must take care of is purchasing insurance for your business. While your first reaction may be that insurance is too expensive, there are insurance companies that have policies designed for small business and priced accordingly. There are many different types of liability insurances that you can buy for your company. But which ones do you need?

→ *Commercial Property Insurance* protects the company if property is lost, damaged or stolen. Generally it covers the cost to repair damaged property and replace lost property. You may be able to get named-peril policies which protect the company against losses resulting from the specific perils named in the policy such as fire, or all-risk policies which protect against all perils except those specifically excluded. Other issues for you to consider are the amount of the deductible, whether you need business interruption insurance, flood or earth-quake insurance, or whether you have vehicles to cover, or need insurance to cover products in transit.

→ *Liability Insurance* covers damages that the company causes to other persons for such things as personal injuries, bodily injury, and property damage. This type of insurance includes products liability insurance.

→ *Umbrella Policy* is excess liability insurance providing catastrophe protection which kicks in after the primary insurance is exhausted.

→ *Workers Compensation* is required by law and pays for work-related injuries suffered by employees on the job.

→ *Directors and Officers Liability* protects members of the board of directors and officers of the business against "wrongful acts" claims by an assortment of claimants including shareholders, competitors, governmental entities, etc. Also, it is very common for outside members on your board of directors to require this type of insurance as a condition of their service.

→ *Employment Practices* covers the company if it is sued over things like sexual harassment, discrimination, and wrongful discharge.

→ *Employee Dishonesty* protects against theft of money or property by employees.

Step 10: Business Startup Steps

10.1 Setting up Your Company – Let's Go Shopping

This isn't the sexiest part of creating the business, but we'll show how to squeeze value in the most mundane places – from renting office space to offering credit. The key, as you'll see, is to spend no more than you budgeted for. Actually, you'd prefer to spend less than you projected and cut costs as much as possible without negatively impacting the business. Unspent cash gives you more to use later for growing your business or as a cushion for unforeseen problems or opportunities.

Renting Office Space

If you're not working out of your basement (or garage) you'll need a place to operate your business. The issues regarding location and type of leased space vary considerably based on whether you are a retail business, a service business, or a distribution company.

In a retail business, choosing a location will be the most important decision you make. The decision of where to locate often comes down to the amount of rent you can spend. As you would expect, the best locations will be more expensive than other alternatives. Don't try to trim costs here. A good location is usually worth its weight in gold. There's a reason it is often said, "In retail the top three things that matter most are: location, location, location." If your business relies heavily on walk-in business, a low-cost location will get you out of business quicker. A good location is more than square footage; it's good marketing.

If you are a service business, you need to consider how your offices will be used. If customers are coming in and out of your office, convenience and decor will matter. If, on the other hand, you conduct business primarily at your customers' place of business, location and style will be less important.

If you are a distribution business, you need to make sure you are located close to a highway or other major street. Again, this is a location issue with a different perspective.

Once you've decided the type of space you need, determine your class and size requirements:

→ **Class:** Real estate tends to be divided into categories such as Class A, Class B or Class C space. Prices can vary widely by city or location. The difference is often based on age, amenities available, and location. For example, in metropolitan Atlanta, Ga., Class A will usually go for around $25.00-$30.00/foot per year, where as Class B could average $15.00-20.00/foot per year and Class C can be as little as $5.00-$7.00/foot per year in some cases. In rural Atlanta, Ill., these prices may be half or less.

→ **Size:** Your space needs can be tricky to determine. You're not just building for the company as it is today, but also for tomorrow, and perhaps even a few years from now. Try to predict growth patterns and anticipate future needs. You don't, however, want to spend money holding empty space while you grow. Hedge your bets by taking a reasonable amount of space with an option to add contiguous space if needed. The amount of space you need per person depends on the type of business you have. Manufacturing and distribution require a lot more than does traditional office space. If you're considering office space, you should plan on 200 to 350 square feet per person on average.

After determining how much space you'll need, the type of building, and location, it's time to shop. Here's where the successful entrepreneur's experience really shows. While most entrepreneurs will request the help of a commercial leasing agent to show them the spaces available, the savvier entrepreneur will look at the classifieds for subleases or find a leasing agent who can show them subleases.

A sublease is an office lease where the renter has left early and in most cases is still responsible for the payments. In many cases, it's a large company moving people around, or a company that grew out of its space. Often, they are willing to accept 40-60% of their rent expense. While new ventures can save 50% or more on rent and you might not even have to sign a personal guarantee on the lease, the tradeoff is that this lease expires when the original company's lease expires, and you have to take the office as is. In most cases, this means a 12-30 month term with rent savings of around $10,000 per every 1,000 square feet rented per year.

Furniture and Equipment

Now that you have an office, you will need to get furniture and equipment to sit on and use. This is an area where many first time entrepreneurs err. Your furniture needs to be functional, comfortable, and not fall apart. With money in the bank, many make the mistake of buying new brand-name furniture. Sure it meets the criteria, but what it costs should make your stomach roll. A single middle management office can cost anywhere between $2,500 and $10,000 to furnish. Even the modular cubicles are going to set you back $2,500 to $3,000 per small cube. In addition, new furniture depreciates quicker than a new car.

Your best option might actually be online. Look at eBay, craigslist, and the classified ads and you'll probably find virtually the same furniture as the fine furniture showrooms. They may have a couple of scratches on them, and possiblt even a piece of paint is chipped, but this could yield a 70% savings or more. So spend your money on a furniture repair kit for $10.00 and pocket on average $2,500 per office.

As far as choosing equipment, this time used is not always the best choice. It just depends. In some cases, the "newness" of the equipment won't matter. Copiers are a good example. A new, high-speed super copier that can do everything except brew your coffee can cost upwards of $20,000. eBay is a great site to find deals that will save you thousands of dollars.

If you need to buy new equipment (sometimes you won't be able to avoid it), it is best to lease instead of buying outright. This may seem counterintuitive. True, leasing a computer for three years is going to be much more expensive than just buying it. However, in entrepreneurial ventures you don't necessarily know when you're desperately going to need the cash that you burned on new computers. By leasing them, on the other hand, you are effectively converting these fixed costs into variable costs. The more that you can do this, the more cash you'll have readily available.

Stationary and Business Cards

Managing how you communicate about yourself and the business is critical. Everything you use to talk to the world – from your letterhead down to your business card – delivers a message. Do you know what that message is? Does it help you stand out from the crowd? At this point you're probably wondering what kind of ideas we could possibly have to save money on your letterhead and your business cards. Obviously "used" is not a good option here.

Here's what we suggest: *Don't* try to save money on these. The difference between a fairly ordinary business card and one that really stands out is about $20.00 a box, so go ahead and splurge. The few extra dollars you'll spend here will go a long way in differentiating your company from everyone else. The same thing goes for your letterhead. Adding a little color to your letterhead might be just enough to enhance your company's impression on the minds of your prospects and customers.

The same is true about your website. It must look very professional. Nothing infuriates customers more than a lot of "under construction" web pages.

Another place to differentiate yourself is a logo, but not every business needs one. Will the logo you choose today still send the message you want if your business evolves quickly over the first year and you enter a different market than you expected? If you do choose to go with a logo, make it look professional, and use it consistently within your letterhead, business cards, and website.

Choosing Your Vendors

You will likely have a wide variety of vendors that you will be working with. Take your time, do your homework, and chose the ones that are best for your specific needs and budget.

Banking: Set up a banking relationship as soon as possible. Look around and learn what services the various banks in your area offer and which are the most important to you. If you think that you might need a loan in the future, you are much better off dealing with a local bank than a big national one. At a local bank, with just a little effort, you'll be able to meet the decision makers and begin building a relationship. Spending time to get to know them can pay off handsomely later when you need that loan.

"Here's a tip: When your order checks, have your check numbers start at 5,000 instead of 1,000. This may suggest to the people you do business with that you are not a start-up company."

Michael

Lawyers and Accountants: As much as we try to save money, you will need an accountant and a lawyer. Ask others who have their own businesses for a referral; don't just rely on a name in the Yellow Pages. If you don't have people to ask, you can also use web-based search engines. The most important thing is to make sure the person you hire understands your line of business. Being the brother-in-law of your college roommate's third cousin is not a good reason to hire someone as your lawyer; and, likewise, an outstanding divorce lawyer probably won't be able to give you the best advice on software license agreements. Interview a couple of lawyers before settling to make sure that they have the skill set you need and that you get along.

"An attorney finds himself in front of St. Peter. He tells St. Peter that there must be a mistake: I'm much too young to die. I'm only 47 years old. St. Peter looks down at him and says, "47? According to your billing records, you're at least 125!"

Charlie

The same thing is true with accountants. Using a large national or regional accounting firm can be overkill and it will cost you an arm and a leg. You can find more affordable options through referrals or online. Work with your accountant to set up your financial systems. While QuickBooks and other software packages are very good, your accountant may suggest ways to set up your chart of accounts or set up other reporting features that will serve you even better.

Other Vendor Considerations: The best advice we have is to do your homework in selecting every vendor. It is possible that you will find vendors who can assist your business in areas other than the sale of their product and service. For example:

→ *Some vendors grant credit:* If a vendor is willing to grant payment terms that enable you to make payments 90 or 120 days from the date of delivery, it's as good as an interest free loan. The vendor is unlikely to come out and offer it; you need to ask.

→ *Marketing Allowances:* If you are selling the vendor's products, ask if the vendor provides money for marketing. It is not uncommon for manufacturers in certain industries to provide advertising and marketing funds to those selling their products. Seek out vendors that share the marketing burden.

Granting Credit to Customers

Remember that making it as easy as possible for your customers to buy your product is fundamental to selling your product. One of the best ways to make buying easier for your customers is to provide them with credit terms (just like the ones we suggested you try to get from your vendors). While granting credit can definitely help you to increase your sales (assuming you have a higher priced product), the key is to not do this at the expense of your profit or cash flow. In granting credit to customers, there are a couple of tools that you can use to determine your customers probability of paying you back. Dun & Bradstreet (otherwise knows as D&B) provides credit reports on businesses that you can use to see their history of paying their creditors. Some of the traditional consumer credit bureau agencies like Experian have entered the commercial credit arena. Most of these companies provide (for an extra charge) a credit score that projects how likely a company is to pay its future bills. This is usually a good indicator to use if you're granting credit to commercial customers.

Even though the credit companies have tools to help you determine whether or not to grant credit, they don't have good tools to help you decide just how much credit to grant. To do this yourself, you'll have to rely on previous payment history and analysis of the buyers' financial statements. If granting credit becomes common practice, hire someone with experience.

In retail, and now even in the service industries, companies accept credit cards as a convenience to customers. Of course, there are both positives and negatives in using this practice. On one hand, accepting credit cards generally increases business because it gives customers more payment alternatives. Additionally, since there is an intermediary payer involved, you are no longer at risk of not getting paid. On the other hand, however, there is a cost involved with credit cards called a merchant discount fee. This fee, which is commonly between 2-3% of the price of the purchase, must also be accounted for in your financial projections.

10.2 Hiring Employees – Getting the Best and Brightest

When getting started out, your employee roster might simply read, "Me, myself, and I." But if things go well, before you know it you'll have to hire employees and deal with the numerous complexities that go along with it. While there are endless tips and tools that you can find regarding the hiring of employees, we think the following steps will serve you well:

→ Determine the type of positions needed, the numbers required, timing of new hires, and salaries.

→ Develop a concise job description for each role.

→ Choose advertising – word of mouth, newspaper classifieds, web-based services, networking, headhunters, etc. – according to the type of candidates you seek.

→ Elect the top candidates from the pool of applicants based on the profile you developed for a successful employee.

→ Narrow the list of candidates to a manageable number and conduct telephone interviews to further reduce the candidate pool.

→ Conduct face to face interviews with your top three to five candidates.

→ When you are down to the final two or three candidates, try to check references as best you can. The key is being creative in getting the information you need. You might also want to consider doing a background check on an employee, especially if she is going to be responsible for money or highly confidential information. Caution! Background checks require the written consent of the employee.

Employee Benefits

If your business requires hiring higher-skilled employees, you will find it extremely difficult to attract qualified and attractive candidates without the right combination of employee benefits. Employee benefits (especially health insurance) are prohibitively expensive for companies who have a relatively small number of employees. In addition to offering health insurance, to be competitive today you also have to offer the following benefits: disability insurance, life insurance, a retirement plan (e.g. 401(k) plan); and family leave. So what's a small business to do?

Professional Employer Organizations

We have used and highly recommend using a professional employer organization (PEO) such as Administaff. We personally have had experience using Administaff, (www.administaff.com), the nation's leading PEO in all our small businesses for over ten years now and highly recommend them. PEOs not only help you save money on employee benefits but also handle many of the day to day tasks and headaches associated with human resources. PEOs effectively become your own human resources department which means that, in addition to helping manage benefits and the like, they can help you find, hire, fire, and train employees – just to name a few of their functions.

PEOs become a co-employer of your employees. You pay the PEO an amount equal to the salary and bonus, all employer-based taxes, and a fee that covers both the administrative costs and the costs associated with the benefits package you choose for your employees. Because PEOs have a large employee base, they are able to negotiate favorable costs for employee benefits such as health insurance and are a great way for you to provide employee benefits that you otherwise couldn't afford to get.

A note of caution. It's imperative to only use a credible PEO with a solid track record. Smaller and less reliable PEOs can cause serious problems for a small business. Although it's very rare, there have been cases where a PEO withheld taxes, went into financial trouble, and never paid the government. Unfortunately, the business is still liable for the taxes. That said, a good PEO will save you time, enhance your image among your employees, and ensure that you're complying with the requisite federal and state laws and regulations.

Managing Expectations

A common problem we see, time after time, is the entrepreneur who does a poor job managing the expectations of employees. This inevitably leads to frustrated employees, inter-company friction, and eventually big problems.

To help you manage employee expectations, we offer the following three recommendations:

→ Start with an offer letter. This letter which you give to a potential employee spells out the job in detail, including salary, benefits, vacation, any probationary periods, etc. To make sure your offer letter is not construed as an employment contract, you need to specifically indicate so in the document.

→ Give employees detailed job descriptions. Better yet, have employees work with you to create their job descriptions. You'll have more buy-in on their end for the roles that you jointly agree on. Furthermore, business will run smoother if employees know exactly what they should be doing and how their performance will be measured.

→ Provide each employee with the company's employee manual. This is a manual that sets forth your company's policies on a variety of matters such as:
  - Discrimination in the workplace
  - Sexual harassment
  - Drinking and drugs in the workplace
  - Weapons in the workplace
  - Attendance and tardiness
  - Appearance and demeanor
  - Internet use
  - Privacy expectations

When giving the manual to your employees, require them to sign a statement saying that they received it, reviewed it, and had the opportunity to ask questions. Also, make sure your manual has a disclaimer on the front stating that, "This is not a contract of employment."

Conclusion

Even though we have addressed a wide variety of issues and made a number of recommendations, it is impossible in this book to cover everything. These are the areas where entrepreneurs often spend the least amount of time. Consequently, they often overlook risk management and don't sufficiently protect their business or themselves.

"Success is not final, failure is not fatal:
It is the courage to continue that counts."

- Sir Winston Churchill, Prime Minister of Great Britain

"Success is not the key to happiness. Happiness is the key to
success. If you love what you are doing, you will be successful."

- Albert Schweitzer, Famous Scientist

"You don't get to choose how you're going to die, or when.
You can only decide how you're going to live."

- Joan Baez, Folk Singer

What You Need To Know About the 23 Tips

Just as one of the keys to a successful sale is giving prospects a little
more for their money, we've included 23 Tips from Successful
Entrepreneurs as a little bonus which we believe you will find very
beneficial. These tips come from very successful entrepreneurs that
we have had the pleasure of meeting along the way. We want to thank
everyone who was kind enough to include their tips in our list. We
know that you will take away a number of lessons and ideas from this
compilation, but please take note that there are a number of recurring
themes – there must be a reason for that!

TIP #1: The Wall Street Journal Test

"Every action you take must pass what I call the Wall Street Journal Test. Would you be comfortable having anyone you know reading about your actions, real or perceived, on the cover of the <u>Wall Street Journal</u>? If the answer is maybe or no, think again. If it is yes, fire away. It applies to all decisions. BTW - The easy ones to make are the obvious good and bad ones. It's all the gray ones in between that need to be properly evaluated. It's not always easy, but applying the WSJT is a great indicator."

- Eric W. Hartz, President and CEO, RentBureau, LLC. Formerly: President, Zap Media; LLC; and President, SFNB/S1

TIP #2: Talk To Your Customers

"If you build what they want, then they will buy what you have. I believe that if you ask your customers the right questions, they will tell you what benefits and features they want, the value those features deliver, how they want the solution packaged and implemented, what distribution channels you should use to reach them, what kind of salespeople they would like to have call on them, and how much they will pay. Once you have that information, you have everything you need to be successful."

- Michael Parham, Managing Partner, Catalysta Partners, LLC; Mike has helped launch a number of early stage companies including: InvoiceLink, XcelleNet, MediaBin, Constructware, EquipMD, and Advectis.

TIP #3: Entrepreneurship is a Team Sport

"I have always maintained a simple formula for success in business:

Success = People + Information

It may sound over simplistic but I can't tell you how many businesses I have seen where these crucial components are overlooked. It is one thing for an entrepreneur to have the right leadership skills but if he/she is not surrounded by the right chemistry of people equipped with the appropriate skills for their respective disciplines, the team will not reach their ultimate goals.

Without the best information system delivering accurate information on a timely basis, success will always elude them. It's like flying without radar."

- Byron Kopman, Executive Director, Schnitzer Southeast, LLC. Formerly: Managing Partner Regional Recycling, LLC; and CEO Mindis Metals, LLC.

TIP #4: Call Me Stupid

"I want to be the dumbest person in the room when it comes to my managers."

- Gerald Benjamin, Managing Director, Corporate Finance, Navigant Capital Advisors, LLC. Formerly: Senior Managing Director, Casa Benjamin and White, LLC

TIP #5: Use the Success Test

"We use the following to screen technologies and start companies:

1. Accomplished people - those with a track record of success – "bet on the jockey, not the horse"
2. Products with high barriers to entry – usually such things as strong patents, but could be something else that keeps competitors out
3. Large profit margins - help to solve the inevitable managerial errors that occur in early stages
4. High societal impact - typically helps in translating to angle investors that have a desire not just to make money but to also have a societal impact
5. Long product life cycles in large product markets – helps justify the cost to starting the business
6. Obviousness - if you cannot explain it or understand it, it is going to be difficult to raise capital and have people understand what you are doing
7. Ahead of its time - close to the others but we do not want to be in the market with 'me too' products"

- Steve Gorlin, founded the following companies: Theragenics, Medicis Pharmaceutical, EntreMed, CytRx, CytRx Biopool, Surgi-Vision, DARA BioSciences, SpineMedica and the MiMedx.

TIP #6: Don't Wait

"1) Surround yourself with smart people that always make you look smarter and 2) do it now, procrastinators always in our experience lose."

- Stanley Tanger, Chairman of the Board/Chief Executive Officer Tanger Factory Outlet Centers, Inc.

TIP #7: Seek Out Great Mentors

"Mentors were a major reason for my success. The smartest thing an entrepreneur can do is to build a network of mentors. Mentors are people that have achieved extraordinary business success and possess the most valuable tool... wisdom. Mentors can help you see opportunities/risks in a different way, and develop a plan to capitalize on opportunities. By leveraging your mentors' experience you can rapidly accelerate your own growth and success.

As I grew up in the business world, I was fortunate to have several tremendous mentors. One was a high ranking military officer who taught me delegation skills, management, leadership and organizational structure. Another mentor was an immensely successful architect/builder who taught me how to organize projects and plans, dissect business opportunities, and turn them into bite-sized actionable steps. These same mentors helped me develop as a business person, meet people, raise money for my businesses and recruit senior talent. Their influence and impact on my life is immeasurable.

How do you meet a mentor and build a relationship? By their nature, mentors tend to be very successful, very wealthy, older and often hard to meet. As a young business person, I had a client who was a retired Colonel and very impressive. I merely asked him to have lunch with me because I knew he had wisdom that would be incredibly helpful. I had nothing to offer this man other than my friendship, appreciation and loyalty. I never asked him for money, only his friendship and wisdom. Remember that sincerity shines through. I have found that mentors are naturally drawn to energy and enthusiasm and hope."

- David Zalik, CEO, GreenSky Financial, CEO, Outweb, Inc. and co-founded Phoenix, LLC. Formerly: CEO, MicroTech Information Systems

TIP #8: Show Me the Money!

"Cash is King. Become an expert in knowing where and how your cash is being generated and consumed in your business. A common misstep is to leave this task to your bookkeeper or CPA. Completely understanding how your cash flows through your business model is the key to survival first, and then growth."

-   Ed Rieker, PbNation, LLC. Formerly: Enroll Link, Inc. Officemed, LLC, and Nation Verification Systems, LLC.

TIP #9: Never Give Up... Unless It's Time To Quit

"First remember the paradox of entrepreneurship.

Combine the determination of Churchill's never, never, never give in with the difficult insight of knowing when to quit. In other words, give your business your all, but don't let it destroy you if it is failing.

Second, don't forget the impact of the business on your family and don't underestimate the impact your family can have on the business. That impact can be large and positive, or devastating. To a big extent, it's up to you to make the experience of entrepreneurship a positive one for your family and keep them an asset to your success. Remember that an entrepreneur is always selling, even to your family. But it goes beyond sales. Your family must not view the business as the enemy that takes you away from them. Rather they must view it as a realistic source of tangible reward for them all."

-   Robert (Bert) Jones, Chairman, Accucast, Inc. Formerly: Chairman, Sedoa Systems, Inc. and President, Strategic Solutions Group, LLC

TIP #10: Run Like The Wind

"When you get that amazing insight for your business and you Google it and there's nothing there already, be very certain of one inevitable truth. There are at least 15 others with equal or better intelligence, equal or better relationships in the space and more money. So, you have to move faster which means bring that service/product to those customers FAST. Do not study it to death. An entrepreneur is ready, fire. The rest of Corporate America is ready, aim, aim, aim..... you get my point."

- Harold Solomon, Co-founder RentBureau. Formerly: Co-founder: Seraphim Partners; Co-founder TeleKey, and Co-founder, Mercury Communications

TIP #11: Be Tough – This Stuff is Hard

"A major key to success for entrepreneurs is determination and attitude. Starting your own business is easy; being successful and surviving to year 3 and beyond is much harder. Success requires putting your customers FIRST in everything you do. Your customer's support is what feeds you. You must build a team of people who share your goals and follow your lead. Choose people who are truly honest, pay them fairly; share your success with them. You must understand you cannot do everything yourself. Everyday no matter how hard it looks or feels you have to remain focused on your goals. Your attitude sets the tone for your entire team. You have to be up when they are down, you need to see problems as opportunities and most of all you need to learn from yours and others mistakes."

- Dean Benamy; Founder and CEO, The Houseboat Store LLC; CEO Benamy International Inc., CEO Houseworks, LTD

TIP #12: Treat Employees Like Customers
and Customers Like Kings

"Here are my tips on running a successful business, and which we have tried to follow throughout our 37 years of operation. Some we followed from the onset, others we picked up on fairly quickly through revelations.

1. Treat other people the way you want to be treated (customers, employees, suppliers, etc.).
2. Always operate with honesty and integrity.
3. Surround yourself with great people.
4. Offer only the highest quality products and/or service.
5. Treat your customers and suppliers as if they were special, they are.
6. Respond to your customers' needs as your business depends on it, it does.
7. Be flexible in your operations (policies, procedures, etc.) but hold your people and yourself to the highest standards.
8. Show your customers that you appreciate their business. Nobody appreciates being taken for granted.
9. Stay humble (Success without Humility is Failure).
10. Treat your employees with respect and they will treat you with the same.
11. Take care of your employees and they will take care of you.
12. Offer a benefits package to your employees that is second to none.
13. Be genuinely interested in your employee's welfare, and also that of their family.
14. Maintain a nice business environment in which to operate."

-    L. Gary Ashley, President, Conveyors & Drives, Inc.

TIP #13: Lead, Follow, or Get Out Of The Way

"To be successful in business today, everyone needs an entrepreneurial skill set. In a very dynamic, international, regulatory focused business environment, the greatest challenge is to balance all these facets and attract a great work force. Leading a company means leading your work force. Having a clear measurable goal for company performance and individual reward is core to retention and attraction of what makes a difference - your employees. WRS is a 23 year proven green environmental construction company that is proud of its safety record and client relationships."

- Kathleen Shanahan, CEO, WRS Infrastructure & Environment, Inc.

TIP #14: The First Step's A Doozy:

"The hardest part of being an entrepreneur is what I call 'the leap. Most of our lives we're on a track: high school leads to college, college leads to a first job, a first job leads to a better job, etc. Every entrepreneur at some point "leaps" off this track and trades a predictable career path for the much riskier life of an entrepreneur. The good news is once you've actually taken the leap, your fear transforms into a laser focus on what you need to do to be successful."

- Jared Hyman, Founder and President, Infosurv, LLC

TIP #15: Stay Alert and Stay Focused to Stay In The Game

"The following are some of the important lessons I've learned in building my business:

1. Build a great team – internal and external;
2. Give your people a stake in the future;
3. Communicate with all your stakeholders give them the good and bad news;
4. View systems as a primary competitive advantage;
5. Don't fall in love with your business model, it will change;
6. Running scared is running right;
7. Make sure your people know the rules so they can break them properly;
8. Understand your core competencies; and
9. The only time we don't make mistakes is when we are sleeping."

   \-   Rob Perkins, CEO, Value Music Concepts

TIP #16: One Thing At A Time
"You can do anything you want to do,
but you can't do everything."

   \-   James Davis, CEO, TerraGo Technologies; Formerly: President, Harbinger Net Services

TIP #17: Be Confident, But Not Foolish

"Here are some tips to assist:

→   Have the confidence to always believe you are right, but the humility to listen and change direction when you are proven wrong;

→   Rarely accept NO, and creatively and aggressively figure out how to change a NO to a YES;

→   Trust your instincts and your gut to do things others do not believe are possible;

→   Always think and project positive thoughts because it is contagious;

→ Make your own luck by working harder and being smarter than your competition; and

→ Under-commit and over-perform."

- Garrett Van de Grift, Chief Executive Officer, Enterprise Vending Group; Vending Management Consultants; Vending Corporation of America; Pine Leaf Management; Suzuki Village; Suzuki School; and WasteILogix

TIP #18: Speed Kills

"The Bucket Race.... I often compare my business to a race where each participant has to carry two buckets full of water to the finish line. The object is to finish the race as quickly as possible AND retain as much water in the bucket as possible. If you run real fast you may be first to the finish line but have no water in the bucket. If you try to retain all the water, you will finish last in the race."

- Bob Wilensky, CEO, AmSouth Mortgage Company. Formerly: CEO, Gulf States Mortgage

TIP #19: Life's Short: Be Competitive and Have Fun

"Do something even if it is the right thing to do." (This probably needs some explaining.)

"The right management team is critical to the entrepreneur. I have always tried to choose people who are competent, competitive, and are fun to be around. Your management team needs to have skills that compliment your own."

- Michael Fletcher, CEO of ULQ. Formerly: CEO of National Action Financial Services, and President and CEO of Debt Collectors Inc.

<u>TIP #20: Nothing Happens Until A Sale Is Made</u>

→ "Persistence – There is no substitute for it and nothing happens until the sale is made – the most modern plant in the world doesn't run until a sale is made.

→ Most start-up problems are solved through sales growth.

→ Make sure you know your true costs.

→ Poor financial support (surprises) can kill a young company.

→ Don't be afraid to 'overpay', if necessary to close – otherwise you may never get started.

→ Learn to let "momentum" close a transaction (sale)."

- Jack Karcher, Founder and CEO of PL Industries

<u>Tip #21: It's Not About the Money, Really!</u>
"What is an Entrepreneur? Big question.

1. First, you must love what you are doing or attempting to do and be totally dedicated. If getting rich is your only goal – forget it.
2. There should be a demand for your product or service.
3. You will have to work hard and then work harder.
4. You must be honest. Tell the truth and you'll never have to change your story.
5. Don't be satisfied with a better mouse trap – you goal must always be to build the best mouse trap.
6. If you have a partner in marriage or a significant other – they must be fast to listen and slow to speak.
7. Remember, it's easier to carry money from the bank than it is to return it.
8. Don't throw money at a project – use thought first.
9. Never become complacent.
10. Always have a goal to achieve – then set another. You must always have a plan. Don't accept defeat.

11. Remember, you are a person wearing many hats at the same time. (Enjoy)
12. Be a dreamer – but dream realistically."

- Frank Leonard, Founder, Chairman, CEO and Sole Shareholder, Electro-Mechanical Corporation

Tip #22: Your Sweat's Not Perfume

"Here are the things I have found valuable in starting a business:
- → Be enthusiastic
- → Have a vision with some barrier to entry
- → Raise enough capital to execute your vision
- → Be persistent
- → Hire great people
- → Remember everything is marketing

And this from Ace Greenberg, "Don't ever start believing your sweat is perfume."

- Eddie Mendel, Co-Founder and Partner, Ned Davis Research Group and Davis, Mendel & Regenstein, Inc.

Tip #23: Customers Buy From Friends

"Points that I have found invaluable in building my businesses:
- → It's not what you know but who you know; friends buy from friends;
- → Become involved in your trade profession;
- → Become involved in your client's trade professions;
- → If you sell locally, get involved in your local Chamber of Commerce; and
- → Always be building your Rolodex – remember you are no more than six degrees of separation from anyone you want to meet."

- Randall Bentley; CEO, Ceramyx, Inc. Formerly: CEO, Platinum Services, Inc.

INDEX